basic Keyboard
Workout

G000108619

Printed in the United Kingdom by MPG Books Ltd, Bodmin

Published by SMT, an imprint of Sanctuary Publishing Limited, Sanctuary House, 45-53 Sinclair Road, London W14 0NS, United Kingdom

www.sanctuarypublishing.com

ISBN: 1-84492-041-0

basic Keyboard Workout

John Dutton

smt

CONTENTS

FOREWORD

Welcome to *basic Keyboard Workout*. This book is designed to give you useful information all the way through, to help you explore and have fun.

The intention is to make as much of the book as useful as possible, whether you have only the most basic understanding of keyboard playing or you've been making music for a while and you want to fill in gaps you've skipped over. I know many good players who have missed important areas of basic knowledge, so take your time and look at even those areas of the book that you might not feel are relevant at first.

What I won't do is take up your time with endless chapters on theory which you can't connect with your music. However, some theory is useful, enabling you to understand – as much as possible – *why* certain things happen. Although all of these pieces of information might take a while to click, things often suddenly slot into place in your mind. For this to happen, however, you've got to keep at it; worthwhile improvements can take time.

basic Keyboard Workout

The book also deals more with using and getting the most out of your equipment and handling different playing situations. Making full use of whatever gear you've got can transform your playing experience and your enjoyment of music. So, even though you might tread the waters of modern technology a bit uneasily, it really is pretty simple to hook up a keyboard to a computer, for instance, and start opening up a whole new world of making music.

I'm a firm believer in all knowledge being useful; the more you know about something, the more enjoyment you get out of it. Music is music, after all, so enjoy it all.

Part 1

Playing Your Keyboard

1 POSTURE

First reaction: skip this chapter. Right? After all, what has posture really got to do with playing, when it comes down to it? Either you can play or you can't.

Well, posture has quite a lot to do with playing, actually. In fact, a hell of a lot. However, what I won't do is get you hung up on the subject and give you so many instructions that playing is the last thing on your mind. What I want to do is to make you think, and to apply that thought in such a way that it becomes second nature. After a while you'll realise that it doesn't only benefit your playing, it makes you enjoy it more. And that's what counts, period.

Sitting Or Standing?

You may prefer (or be required) to stand and play on-stage. It usually looks more dynamic and may well improve your chances of pulling at the gig. However, I sometimes think that the only reason keyboard players stand on-stage is because they can. A drummer couldn't play effectively standing up (although Keith Moon had a good go sometimes!), and likewise for a keyboard player, in terms of ideal playing positions, sitting is better.

I'm not going to ignore the needs of players who stand – in fact, they well may be in more need of help. Firstly, though, I shall concentrate on the sitting position because that's where most of your playing time will be spent, whether practising or recording.

The Youth Of Today...

Question: Can you remember how many times you were told to sit up straight at school? And when you went home you probably slouched in front of the TV as well...

Over the years, it's easy to get into a habit of sitting in a certain way, and it could be responsible for problems in everyday life. When you sit (or stand) in a static position for any length of time, you become much more aware of the effects of bad posture. If you drive, for instance, you'll know that, after a few hours at the wheel in some cars, backache creeps in, and it can get very uncomfortable indeed, often due to a lack of support in the seat or a poor driving position.

When you play your keyboard, you don't want to be bothered by backache – a poor position will also compromise your playing ability. The habits I described above can lead to you setting up your gear to work around the situation, which won't help you in time. Believe me, I know a lot of musicians – not necessarily just keyboard players, either – who have had problems relating to the way in which they stand at, sit at or hold their instruments. Sometimes, it unfortunately takes something dramatic to make people change their ways. However, I don't want you to have to do it the hard way and have problems with posture limit your enjoyment of the music. That's the last thing you want. So, without getting into intricate detail, let's bear in mind a few factors that will hopefully help you play in a comfortable way and give you a good technical base to work from.

Sitting Down

An acoustic piano's keyboard is usually around 28 inches/71cm off the ground. If you own an electric piano resting on a tailor-made stand, the chances are it will be roughly the same height, as will a typical X-frame stand for a synth at its lowest position. I'd make this your starting point.

Next, use a chair (without arms) or stool that has a decent depth to the seat. The idea is not to sit right back onto it but towards the front end so that the weight of your body is firmly on your bottom. The seat must also be flat and firm – don't waste time with something that's soft or sinks in the middle.

When you sit down to play, think about the angle of your back – it should be running straight from the head down to the bottom. Let the weight sink onto your bottom, but not at the expense of arching your back. Your feet should be able to reach the floor comfortably, with the heels lightly taking a natural amount of weight. If you use a sustain pedal, this is especially important, as the heel is used as a pivot for the rest of the foot to depress and release the pedal.

Many people play while sitting (or standing) too high. Perching too high will encourage you to slouch and arch your back, which can lead to a whole range of problems. Accompanying this is a resultant tendency to drop the head down to look at the keyboard or read music. This really is bad news. If it's a habit you have, try to get out of it as soon as possible. Don't forget that your eyes are designed to move in your head – if you let them do the work, there's usually no need to look down. If you haven't got one, buy a decent stool at a good height and get used to it, so that you play in the same position wherever you go.

Now, all of this may give you the impression that you sit at the keyboard dead still, fearful of moving a muscle in case you move to the wrong position. This is emphatically not the case. If you move around a lot when you play, that's fine. Instead, regard the advice above as general information to store and be used if it works for you.

Standing

Playing standing up brings its own set of issues. Unless (or even if) an X-frame stand is set really high, you're likely to end up crouched over the keyboard with your head bent down – as we've seen, not good. An A-frame or other vertical-bar stand is a common choice, particularly if you're using more than one keyboard. That's OK, although you may need to reappraise how high the keyboard actually has to be, remembering that the same things apply as when sitting down. It's no use having a keyboard set at waist height and expecting to be able to play anything. People do, but it's unnecessary, uncomfortable and it severely limits playing ability. Instead try having the keyboard much nearer chest height so you can adopt a more natural position. Don't use the keyboard to lean on, either – stand up with your back as straight as possible and play the instrument without using it to prop yourself up. (A note of caution: if you are putting a single keyboard higher than usual, be careful that the stand doesn't become top-heavy and crash to the ground.)

basic Keyboard Workout

When using a sustain pedal while sitting, body weight rests on the bottom and the heel is used as a pivot, as described above. However, when standing up, your feet are used to take the weight of your body and also balance it. This means that you need to bring the pedal closer than usual or you'll adopt an extremely awkward position with the pedal too far underneath the keyboard. A good idea is to gaffer-tape the pedal in position on-stage so it doesn't move. This can still be a bit awkward, as you partially lose balance when weight gets taken off the toes, and if this is noticeable you should make sure that the backs of your knees aren't locked tight, sagging them slightly to help you balance.

As we explore basic playing technique, the benefits of good playing posture will become more apparent. In time you'll regard it almost as a good friend, as you'll be relaxed and it will help to advance your playing more than you realise.

If you're interested in learning more about posture, it could be worthwhile checking out the Alexander technique, which is used by many musicians and actors to help them to relax and perform to their maximum on-stage. Contact details can be found easily on the Internet.

2 BASIC TECHNIQUE

Technique – another subject that's often misunderstood.
On hearing someone perform a flashy run, it's natural
to remark, 'Oh, what a wonderful technique.' That's
missing the point, really. It's not just what the player
is doing in terms of making the sound, it depends on
how he or she is achieving it. The player in question
might not necessarily have a good technique at all; he
or she might just be comfortable with that particular
run, or holding tension, adopting bad habits and so
on in order to be able to do it. Technique goes far, far
deeper than appearing to be able to execute a quick
run or something similarly flashy – it's something that
is at the very core of your playing. Providing you keep
up your facility on the instrument, you should never
lose it, only improve.

We've looked briefly at how posture and the way you
sit or stand at the keyboard has an important effect on
playing. That is perhaps the most basic form of
technique in itself – it's allowing you to have the base
to work from in order to progress. The best explanation

I have for describing technique, and what it means to your playing, is the ability of your body to do any task that your mind sets it in as efficiently and effortlessly as possible. It doesn't require a great deal of effort to play a keyboard, any more than a boxer with a knockout punch hits particularly hard. Instead, it's finding the important elements and getting them working in an effective – yet simple – way.

Technical ability can be measured at different levels. The important thing is that firstly you become comfortable within the musical area you're in now, be it beginner or more advanced. There is actually nothing wrong with having a simple yet effective technique, depending on the kind of music you want to play – it's far better to play something simple properly than trying to clatter through a more complicated part and never getting it right. Of course, I want you to set your goals as high as possible, but this should never be at the expense of getting your form right.

Getting Your Form Right

Sit down at the keyboard as near to the middle as possible, close enough to allow the fingers to reach well towards the backs of the keys. Now put your hands on the keyboard. The elbows should naturally push outwards slightly – certainly don't make an effort to hold them in against the body. The wrist should be relaxed and straight with the forearm – don't allow it to drop or push up. Bend the fingers so that the tips are in contact with the keyboard and slightly bent. The hand should now create an arch. An old favourite among piano teachers was to allow a pencil to be put through the arch underneath the hand. This can encourage a wrist position that's slightly too high, but it's a useful starting point to gauge basic hand position. Long fingernails make it difficult to keep the fingers bent – the little pad at the top of your finger should be the part that makes contact with the keys. If you can hear your fingernails clattering, it's best to get them cut, I'm afraid.

Just sit and think how things feel for a moment. It's quite common for wrists to hold quite a bit of tension. Without allowing them to drop down, consciously allow them to relax as much as possible. When you do this, you may become aware of a little more weight falling onto the fingertips. That's good. Hold the position without playing for a few seconds and remember the feeling.

We need to now perform some simple exercises to help get this form we've created into our minds. These particular exercises are based around *scales* and *arpeggios* – the nuts and bolts of music.

With each exercise and piece of music that follows, there will be a reference to fingering in the form of numbers from 1–5. To avoid any doubt, 1 indicates thumb, 5 indicates little finger and 2, 3 and 4 represent the fingers in between.

Keyboard Orientation

When I said to sit as near to the middle of the keyboard as possible, that's for a few reasons (some which are pretty obvious). Obviously, it means that you can reach to the extreme right or left of the keyboard with the relevant hand, and therefore cover all of the available notes. It also means (in the context of a piano keyboard, at least) that you're sitting near to a note called *middle C*. Middle C is perhaps the most relevant point of reference you can have on a piano-type keyboard. While it is not a dividing line as such between the areas that the right and left hands play in, you're likely to play more with your right hand in the area from middle C upwards (higher) than your left, and conversely in the area downwards from middle C (lower) more with your left than with your right.

There is a possible complication with this on an electronic keyboard. A piano usually comes with an 88-note keyboard (full length) and is not transposable. Middle C is therefore always in the same physical position on the keyboard (between the two pedals).

A synthesiser may have a much shorter keyboard and a C in the middle of the keyboard may not be at the same pitch as that on a piano. In other words, it could be playing a higher (or lower) C. On most keyboards, this can be changed easily.

Playing A Basic Exercise

Put your right hand onto the keyboard as described in the section above and place your thumb on middle C. The centre joint of the thumb should have a slight bend outwards. Now place the other fingers onto each subsequent white note, travelling up the keyboard – D, E, F, G. Remember to keep that arch formed with your hand. Now, while keeping that arched hand position intact and making sure your wrist is relaxed, lift your thumb up slightly and depress it to sound the note of middle C. While you're doing this, keep the other fingers resting lightly on or as close to the keyboard as possible – you may find this difficult initially, but it will become easier with time.

Bring up the thumb to release the note and at the same time lift up and depress the second finger to play the next note so that, as one is released, the next is played. There should be no audible gap between the two notes – but no overlap, either. This style of playing is called

basic Keyboard Workout

legato, an Italian word meaning 'smoothly'. Continue along with the sequence in this legato manner until you've played G with your little finger, then play the notes back down again to middle C.

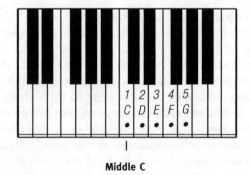

Middle C

Let's play the left hand on its own. Place your little finger on the next C down, an *octave* beneath middle C, and the other four fingers on each following white note, just as you did with the right hand. Follow the same procedure to play legato-fashion up to the G and back down again, making sure the wrist is relaxed and the hand remains arched. Repeat this with both hands separately a few times, remembering how it feels, and then try both hands together.

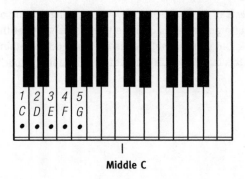

Middle C

This exercise should be played slowly – listen to the CD for an example of how it should sound. Try to reach the bottom of each note – don't skate on the tops of the notes so that they don't fully sound.

This exercise may be basic, but it's also extremely valuable. Irrespective of your playing level, it's always useful to sit down for a few minutes and pay attention to posture and basic technique like this. In this way, when you're in a playing or performing situation, you'll find that your body has retained a lot of this physical information and you won't have to be aware of it as much. It will really help, though, if you do this for at least a few minutes every day – especially at first – to get used to your playing position and these basic

27

aspects of playing technique. I'm not going to bang on about practice levels and the like at this stage of the book, but you will feel the results if you do something like this every day. Little and often is a good approach.

3 BASIC EXERCISES

So far we've looked at how valuable basic posture and technique are. But when are we actually going to play something and apply this musically?

Well, the exercise we did in the last chapter is a more relevant musical exercise than you might think. Indeed, all rudimentary exercises such as scales and arpeggios are, and that's the way you should think of them. Sometimes this is not apparent straight away, so to give you an example before we move on, I'm going to show you a basic chord born out of that last exercise.

Place both of your hands on the keyboard in the same position as for the previous exercise. We played five notes in a row, from C to G, with both hands, each note played separately. I'm going to show you how to play a major chord without having to change your hand position. Let's take the right hand on its own first. Instead of playing the sequence from C to G in separate notes as before, locate the position of your thumb, third and fifth fingers, which should be resting (but not playing) the notes of C, E and G respectively. Then I want you to lift up the hand – with a relaxed wrist, of course – and play those three notes at the same time. When you lift up the hand, you may raise the wrist slightly, allowing it to return to its normal angle – parallel to the floor – once the chord has sounded.

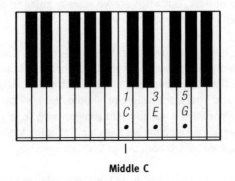

Middle C

The dots mark the notes you should play, with middle C marked so you can orientate yourself on the keyboard. The fingering is indicated above the respective note name.

With your left hand, locate the notes of C and G only with your fifth finger and thumb in the same position as the last exercise, then lift up the hand with a relaxed wrist and play those two notes at the same time.

For maximum effect, both hands should be played together. Make sure that each finger reaches the bottom of its respective note to ensure that it sounds properly.

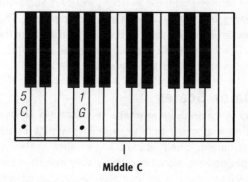

Middle C

This arrangement of notes is also called a C major *triad* (three notes). Thousands of well-known songs start with this chord – think of John Lennon's 'Imagine' or Oasis's 'Don't Look Back In Anger', to name a couple.

Why don't you play three notes in the left hand as well as the right? Well, you can try playing the E with your

31

third finger as well to mirror what you do with your right hand, but I think you'll agree that, when you play both hands together, it sounds tighter and cleaner with only those two notes sounding in the left hand. We'll cover voicings such as this, and why they matter, in a later chapter.

You can see that these exercises will have some direct bearing on things you're likely to end up playing. That's how I'd like you to think of them, as well as using them to hone your basic technique, because playing an instrument is about making music, after all.

Major Scales

You may already know what a major scale is. However, I find that many pupils, even if they play another instrument, don't always know what scales and arpeggios are. More importantly, they haven't realised how important it is for their playing and understanding of music to have a proper grasp of them. So, even though we're going to start off with a basic C major scale, I'd urge you to follow this through (it won't take long), as scales are also excellent for warming up.

The five-note exercise we've already performed comprises just over half of a C major scale. We're now going to learn all of it.

Right hand only first. Find the same hand position you performed the previous exercise in, with your thumb on middle C and your other fingers resting lightly over the next four notes, up to G. Now play the first three notes – C, D and E – with thumb, second and third finger as before. After you've played the E, however, instead of playing F with the fourth finger, tuck your thumb under the arch of the hand to play the F. It's normal for beginners to find the wrist and forearm pushing out at an angle to help this happen – it can be a bit awkward at first. As much as you can, though, keep your hand in the same arched position and keep the sound legato, as you did in the previous exercise, trying to play that F with the thumb at the same time as releasing the previous note.

Once the thumb is on the F, you'll see that you can play the next four notes without having to change hand position again, up to where the little finger plays C an octave above middle C. That's a complete ascending (ie going up) C major scale. To come down again (ie to descend), just reverse the process, as shown in the diagram at the top of the next page. After having played F with the thumb, put the third finger over to the E and follow down to middle C with your second finger and thumb. That transition with the thumb is a bit easier coming down.

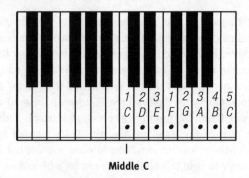

Middle C

Next, try it with the left hand, as shown below. Again, start on the C an octave down from middle C with your fifth finger on the C. When you've reached the G with your thumb, move your third finger over the top to play

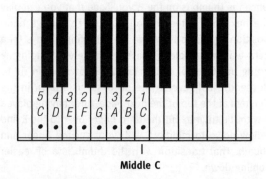

Middle C

34

the A and use your second finger and thumb on the B and C respectively. Coming down is again a reverse process (although you may find it a little more awkward coming down, as the thumb has to be tucked under to play the G).

Now it's time for the logical conclusion to these exercises – both hands together. Again, find the starting position with both hands on the keyboard. As you've seen when playing both hands individually, the hand positions change at different points. When ascending the keyboard, the right-hand thumb tucks under for the F and the left-hand third finger goes over for the A. Coming back down the scale, the order is reversed, with the left-hand thumb now going under for the G and the right-hand third finger crossing over for the E. Some people grasp this more quickly than others, but if it takes a little practice, stick at it because it's an invaluable sequence to learn. The same fingering is used for many major and minor scales and will help greatly when you need to perform quick runs and other, more advanced, passages.

Major Arpeggios

Arpeggios are exercises like scales, but they are formed around the structures of chords. Remember the C major chord you just played? Well, you can see that the chord is formed by taking the first, third and fifth notes of the C major scale – C, E and G. Well, a C major arpeggio is based around just these three notes, plus another C at the octave above. Taking the right hand first, it looks like this:

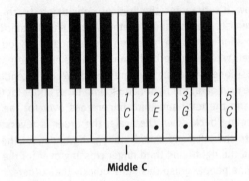

Middle C

Try to keep your hand in the same position when you play this arpeggio – make sure the wrist is relaxed and don't let it rotate noticeably, although a certain amount of movement is OK. The left-hand part turns up like the diagram at the top of the next page.

When you're comfortable with each hand individually, perform the exercise with both hands together. It's often easier than a scale, as there's no thumb to tuck under

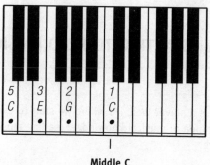

Middle C

at the moment. Remember to treat these exercises not as a chore but as a valuable tool for warming up and improving your general dexterity.

4 STARTING TO READ MUSIC

What is a stave? Well, it's where we start to explore a major area of musical knowledge: reading music from a page.

In my opinion, reading music is of enormous benefit. Lots of very fine professional players don't read, instead relying on their hearing of music (playing by ear) as their main tool. However, many of them honestly wish that they *did* read music but consider it too late to be able to relate it to their playing. Certainly, to have a good musical ear – to be able to identify chords and interpret music without having it written down – is extremely important, but it shouldn't be an either/or situation. The most beneficial way of learning to read music is at the same time as you develop your playing and hearing skills, so that you can think of them all as one. There are sometimes negative prejudices surrounding musicians who read, usually held by those who can't. Forget them. Providing you use it in the right way – as a complement to your playing – an ability to read music can only be to your advantage. The fewer gaps you have in your understanding of music, the more you'll get out of it. Guaranteed.

Music is written down on *staves*, which are groups of five horizontal lines linked together. If you look at a typical piece of keyboard music, it will have two staves placed together. The top one is for the right hand, the lower for the left. Each stave (or staff) has five lines and will have a symbol such as 𝄞 (treble clef) or 𝄢 (bass clef) at the start. When you see a treble clef, it usually relates to the right hand; the bass clef refers to the left. Hence usually the treble clef will be at the start of the top, right-hand stave, and the bass clef will be at the start of the bottom, left-hand stave. There are exceptions, but we'll come to those later.

Taking the treble clef first, I'll show you how what we've already done is written down. Firstly, let's see what middle C looks like:

basic Keyboard Workout

The right-hand part of the scale of C major, which you've already played, looks like this:

Here's middle C on the bass-clef stave along with the left-hand part of C major scale:

Both hands together, therefore, looks like this:

The C major chord we played looks like this:

It's pretty easy to see how notes on the stave relate to the keyboard. This scale, as written, relates only to a certain area on the stave. The diagram below gives a more comprehensive guide:

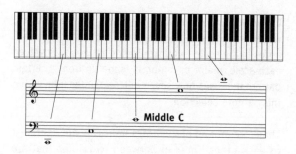

Looks pretty straightforward? It is. It takes time, though, before you know instinctively how the notes on a stave relate to their positions on a keyboard. My priority is to get you playing something as quickly as possible, understanding what you're doing on the way. This is best done by playing pieces of music, so I'm going to press on with that in mind. In order to do this, we need to touch on a couple of subjects: keys and rhythm.

Keys And Harmonic Structures

When you played that scale, you played all seven notes in the key of C major. Therefore, all those notes – C, D, E, F, G, A and B – can be said to be in the key of *C major*. The key note in a scale (in this case, C) is also known as the *tonic*.

If you were to count all of the notes, white and black, within an octave – for instance, between the two C notes in the scale – you would find 12, not 7. However, each scale, major or minor, is made up from a certain pattern that uses only seven different notes from within this 12-note selection.

Therefore, not all of the notes in a scale are right next to each other. The gap between two notes that are adjacent to each other is called a *semitone*. Looking at the diagram above, you can see that E to F is a semitone, as is B to C. C to D, though, has a (black) note in between, and the gap (or *interval*) between them is known as a *tone*. Any scale, be it major or minor, is made up of a pattern of *semitones* (also called *halftones*) and tones.

Major scales just happen to have the following order of tones and semitones: tonic (key note), tone, tone, semitone, tone, tone, tone, semitone, tonic. That's what gives them the sound they have.

Each of the 12 notes within an octave has its own scales and key structure. C major is a straightforward choice to start with as it (uniquely) uses only white notes and is easy to remember. For reasons that will become clear, new major keys are covered in a certain order, starting with G.

With your right hand, start on G and use the same fingering as with C major. Follow the white notes up and when you get to F, the last note before you reach the G at the top of the scale, see how it sounds. Your ear may well tell you that something is not quite right somewhere...

Remember what I said about the major scale being made up of a pattern of steps – tone, tone, semitone, tone, tone, tone, semitone? Well, while following that pattern has got us up to F using just white notes, the F itself just doesn't sound right. If you look at the interval between the last two notes (semitone), you have your answer – F isn't right next to G, is it? But the black note in between *is*, and it's called F sharp. Therefore the seventh note of G major scale is F sharp, and F sharp is the key signature of G major.

If you saw this written down, it would be even more apparent. If a note is to be played as a sharp, it is indicated by a sign – ♯ – and G major appears on a stave like this:

I've put the key signature for this scale and all subsequent ones at the start of the staves in front of the scale, which is where you'd expect to see it at the start of a piece of music. Normally when this occurs there would then be no subsequent ♯ sign in front of the note when written, so I've put it in brackets to remind you.

As with C major, try the left hand on its own next and then both hands together when you're confident you can do it. When you've got this under your belt, try the G major arpeggio and chord:

As we're getting through this pretty quickly, the next major key we need to get to know is D major. Whereas G major had one sharp, D major has two. We keep the sharp we've already encountered – F♯ – and we add another. There's a very easy way of finding out what it is...

You'll remember that the last interval before the tonic is reached (between the seventh and eighth notes) is a semitone. That's why G major has an F♯ – it's a semitone below G. So now that we're in the key of D, which has got two sharps, we know already that it's going to have an F sharp in it. (You can confirm that by following through the tone, tone, semitone, tone, tone, semitone pattern.) We know there's a semitone gap between the seventh and eighth notes, so as the eighth note is D, the seventh one must be C♯, the black note directly below D. (The new note to be sharpened in major keys is always the seventh note.)

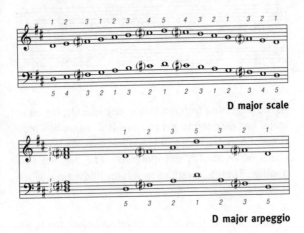

D major scale

D major arpeggio

So, we know three major chords and three major scales: C, G and D.

As we're marching through this, we'll cover another couple of major chords: A, which has three sharps; and E, which has four. Taking A first, we already know that it has F♯ and C♯ already in its key signature. To find the new sharp in a major key, we go to the seventh note

– in this case, G – and sharpen it. The A major triad looks like this:

A major arpeggio

A major scale

Likewise, we know that E major will have F♯, C♯ and G♯ already in its key signature, and to find the new sharp we again go to the seventh note – D – and sharpen that. Have a look over the page:

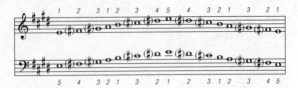

E major scale

E major arpeggio

So now we've got five major chords under our belt –
we know the key signatures for each of them and also
what they look like on paper. I could have told you the
information a bit more quickly than that, but I wanted
you to understand it, hear it and see it all as much as
possible – no gaps, remember?

We're getting close to playing along with a track on the
CD, but first let's look at a few elements of rhythm.

5 BASIC RHYTHM

Rhythm governs our lives. Our hearts beat, keeping us alive, and our bodies naturally respond to external sources of rhythm. Worked around this is the rhythmic structure of music, which in the case of popular music, in particular, is often designed to get your foot tapping, get you jigging along, whatever. It's based around a *pulse*, or a *beat*, the speed of which determines the nature of the track. A good example of a beat is the solid bass-drum part of a typical dance record. It's that constant, relentless thud – often heard through your neighbour's wall or from the open window of a passing car – that drives the track along. What that kind of bass drum part is usually doing is playing along with the pulse of the track, usually in the case of an up-tempo (quick) dance record at about 140bpm (beats per minute). That's quite fast – enough to get you knackered after dancing along for a few numbers! A slower track, such as a ballad, could typically be anywhere from 70–100 beats per minute. In the case of a ballad, you wouldn't have such an audible example as that constant bass drum banging through from start to end, but it would still have a pulse that can be felt running through it.

However, a piece of music has to have a rhythmic structure – a basic framework – within which this pulse, or *beat*, can be placed. Depending on the type of piece, the emphasis, or *feel*, of the beat can also be different. 'Happy Birthday' doesn't feel the same as 'Land Of Hope And Glory', does it?

So we divide these beats up into bars. At extremes, a bar may last anything from 2 to 15 beats, although popular music – including our mythical dance-track example – very often has four beats to the bar. This is known commonly as being 'in four' or 'in four-four' (written 4/4). The number of beats a bar has denotes its *time signature*.

A time signature is represented on a stave as follows:

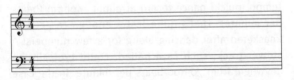

4/4 time signature

Within a bar of music, we need to have a means of explaining when notes should be played and for how long they should last. For a simple example, the bass-drum part described above was being played on every beat, therefore being played four times in a bar. Now, imagine that you wanted to play along with that bass-drum part – say, on middle C – so that what you played sounded at exactly the same time. It would look like this:

Bar of quarter notes (crotchets) on middle C

Each of these dots on the stave represents a beat. The *crotchet* signs ( ) indicate that the note is one beat long. If you wanted to make each note last twice as long, for two beats, it would be written as a *minim*, like this:

A two-bar example of minims would look like this:

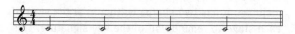

Two-bar example of minims (half notes)

basic Keyboard Workout

Below is a simple piece for you to have a go at. The target tempo of the track is 80bpm, but play it as slowly as you need to while learning:

This track uses four of the chords we've encountered in the book – D, A, C and G major. The piece is in D major, so it has two sharps written in at the start of each stave to remind you of the key signature. This means that any F or C sharps within the following bars don't have to be marked with a ♯ sign. If, for instance, in bars 3 and 7, a C♯ is not to be played (we're playing a C major chord, so that makes sense) a little natural sign (♮) is inserted in front of the relevant note (or notes) indicating that it should be played as a normal, unsharpened C. Once this sign has appeared in front of a note (in this case the C), each subsequent C within that bar is also to be played as a C natural.

At the end of the piece, instead of another line indicating the end of the bar, you will see two bar lines. This is called a *double bar* and it always indicates the end of a piece.

Let's look at the right hand on its own first. As you can see, the piece is in 4/4 and the chords in the right-hand part are all to be played along with the pulse of the track. Use the same fingering – thumb and third and fifth fingers – for each of the chords.

The left-hand part is even more simple: only one note per bar, each lasting for four beats. The fingering is designed so that the hand can stay in the same basic position – it should feel easy to play.

When you're comfortable with playing each hand individually, try both hands together.

basic Keyboard Workout

There is another note value we should understand before moving on. Called either a *quaver* or an *eighth note*, it is half the length of a crotchet (or quarter note). Therefore, two of them make up a beat, and eight of them make up a bar in 4/4. Written singly, they look like this ♪, and if two or more are played one after the other, they are grouped together, as follows:

Two quavers joined

Three quavers joined

Four quavers joined

As a simple exercise, I've written down four tunes in different rhythms below:

More About Time Signatures, Note Values And Rests

Time signatures can be broken down into two distinct types: *simple* and *compound*. Don't worry if this is starting to sound a little complex, because it really isn't! The 4/4 time signature illustrated above is a simple type. The first figure (4) denotes the number of beats in the bar. The second figure (in this case also a 4) refers to the length of beat. When the second figure is

4, it means that the length of a beat is measured as a crotchet, or quarter note.

I mentioned a little while ago about how the emphasis, or feel, of a beat can be different, depending on the type of piece. The 4/4 time signature is very commonly used because it 'feels' easy to listen and play along to. Imagine that dance beat thumping along, and you can count – and feel – the pulse of 4 running through each bar.

Other time signatures, however, can also give music a very distinctive sound, and we'll look at a few of those now.

One time signature that you're likely to audibly recognise is 3/4. Simply, it means (looking at the 3, the first figure) that there are three beats in a bar, with each beat (looking at the 4, the second figure) lasting for a crotchet, or quarter note. The most famous types of pieces in 3/4 time signatures are waltzes, such as 'The Blue Danube'. The English National Anthem and 'Happy Birthday' are other well-known pieces in 3/4. These may be slightly uncool examples, but they illustrate the feel of 3/4 very well.

With familiarity, you can tell 3/4 and 4/4 apart quite easily, such are their different feels. Particularly with

3/4, the slight emphasis on the first beat is helpful when it comes to finding the start of the bar. Try counting out loud along to each time signature – it will help you to recognise them more quickly when you hear them.

We should touch on a time signature in compound time before leaving this section. Compound time sounds a lot more complicated than it actually is – it's only another type of time signature. There is more than one compound time signature, but the only one that we're concerned with right now is 6/8. Thinking back to the explanations behind 4/4 or 3/4 time, we looked at the first number (giving the number of beats in a bar) and the second number (telling us for how long each beat lasts) in turn. Every time signature in the musical world is worked out in this way. So, with 6/8, we know that there are six beats in a bar. The eight refers to the length of each beat, and means eighth notes, or quavers – six beats, each lasting for one quaver.

Why not just have six crotchet (quarter-note) beats in a bar? Well, this time signature is measured in eighth notes to reflect the feel and emphasis of particular pieces. What's more, if it was measured in quarter notes, it would make the tempo very fast. We move into compound time (anything over eight – with an eighth-note pulse – is classed as being in compound time) and measure the pulse in eighth notes for those reasons. But the best way to explain how 6/8 works is to hear it.

Written down, it looks like this:

A simple 6/8 tune

You may recognise the characteristic sound of 6/8 in many well-known pop songs, often slower numbers. Also, you can see that the six quavers are divided up into two groups of three. While together they make up six quavers, these two groups give an emphasis of two in the bar, rather than six.

Rests

Music is obviously not just one long, continuous stream of sound; it has space and periods of silence known as *rests*. Rests are simply indications of areas in a part or piece of music where the composer wants you to stop playing for a defined period. For each of the note values we've learnt so far, there is a rest of an equivalent length – eighth note, quarter note, half note and full note. (There are also shorter notes and variations of existing notes yet to learn.)

The diagrams below show what each of these looks like when written down:

Eighth note and rest   Quarter note and rest   Half note and rest   Full note and rest

Note values and corresponding rests

The tunes below – one in 4/4 and one in 3/4 – feature all of these rests:

5 2 1   2   1 3 5   3   1 3 5   1   4

Short tune in 4/4 with rests

1   2   5   2   3 2 1   3 4 3 2   4   5

Short tune in 3/4 with rests

basic Keyboard Workout

An important and common variation is the use of dotted notes and rests. These are very simple to understand. A dot written after a note, as illustrated below, means that the note value is now half as long again. In other words, referring to this half note, which had a value of two beats, it now has three:

A dotted quarter note or rest has a length of one and a half beats:

A dotted eighth note or rest has a length of three-quarters of a beat:

There are many more forms of note values and rhythms in music, many of which give very definite characteristics to its sound – such as in Latin music, for instance. However, a good grasp of these basics will set you on a long way; everything you learn here can be used as building blocks in the future.

6 MAJOR AND MINOR CHORDS

We'll now have a brief look at further keys: major and minor. However, as I've explained, the purpose of this book is not to be a step-by-step tutorial; instead, I want to encourage you to think and find out a few things for yourself. What I want to do is give you an idea of how and why these things matter, and to have explained the basics so that you can apply the knowledge you've acquired to learn more. I've included a chart with key signatures of major and minor keys for reference at the back of the book, and, after having explained more of the basics about major and minor keys, I'm going to move on to other areas of playing.

More Major Chords

You may have noticed a progression when moving onto the next major key with sharp-based key signatures. For instance, we did C major first (no sharps). To get to the next key, G major, go up the C major scale to the fifth note and you get to G. To find the next key from G, go to the fifth note in the scale, and you get to D.

basic Keyboard Workout

This cycle or process carries on through to the other majors we've covered so far: A and E, and on to B and F♯ majors.

This has still left us with a few more keys to cover. Because of the structure of the 12-note scale, some keys need to have *flats* (indicated by a ♭ sign), rather than sharps, in their key signatures. An example is F major: it follows exactly the same major-scale pattern as before: (tonic) tone, tone, semitone, tone, tone, semitone, (tonic). So that makes the first four notes F, G, A and B♭. Why not A♯, you ask? Because each note in a scale has to have a different letter name – you can't have two 'A' notes – A and A♯, to cite this particular instance.

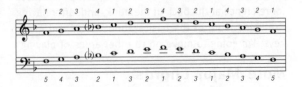

F major scale

F major triad

F major, therefore, has one flat in its key signature: B♭.

Major keys with flat key signatures also have different fingering, and for this reason some people don't bother to learn them. However, it's not difficult and well worth the effort.

To find the next flat key, instead of going to the fifth note of the existing scale, as we did with the sharp-based keys, go to the fourth note instead. The new flat will then be the fourth note of that scale. In the case of F major, the fourth note is B♭. B♭ has two flats in its key signature: B♭ itself and its fourth note, E♭. E♭ major has three flats: B♭, E♭ and its fourth note, A♭ – you get the idea. This process can be followed through to each subsequent flat major key.

Minor Keys And Chords

So far, all of the chords, scales and arpeggios we've encountered have been majors. So what is a minor key?

Well, it's easy to show you, using chords as an example. To play a C major chord, take the first, third and fifth notes of the C major scale – C, E and G – and play them together. To change this to a minor chord, keep the C and G but, instead of playing the E, go one semitone down to the E♭:

63

Cmajor   Cminor

You'll hear the difference between the two straight away. In corny music-lesson parlance, major chords are 'happy' and minor chords are 'sad.' There is some substance to this description as, in contrast to the major chord, the minor does have a more sombre sound. But it's the way in which they're used within music – taking factors such as tempo and phrasing into account – that often gives this impression.

Put simply, the difference between major and minor chords centres on the third note of the scale. A minor chord has what's called a *flattened third* – ie, the third note of the scale is a semitone lower (flatter) than its major counterpart. This is a rule that works with any key.

Minor Scales

A minor scale is similar in many ways to a major one. However, whereas a major scale has semitone gaps between notes 3–4 and 7–8, and follows the interval pattern (tonic), tone, tone, semitone, tone, tone, semitone, (tonic), a minor scale follows a slightly different pattern. We already know that it has a flattened third, so the opening two intervals will be (tonic), tone, semitone. What happens afterwards depends on the type of minor scale you're playing. We'll deal here with the natural (or pure) minor scale.

We'll start with the key of A minor as it shares the same key signature as C major.

Pure A minor scale

When a major and minor key share the same key signature, they are said to be *relative* to each other, so A minor is the *relative minor* to C major. To find the relative minor key from a major, follow the scale of the major key up to the sixth degree to find the tonic of its relative minor. This process can be followed through every key, so once you know the key signature of a major key, its relative minor is easily found. To find the relative major key from a minor, follow the minor scale up to its third note.

basic Keyboard Workout

Using this method, you can very easily find the minor key that has one sharp – for instance, go to G major and go up the scale until the sixth note (E) to find the relative minor key. To find the minor key that has two sharps, go to D major and locate the sixth note of that scale (B). It's pretty simple to work things out this way, and it's always good to know the relationships between related majors and minors.

7 INVERSIONS

To date, every chord we've played in the book has been in what's called *root position*. This is the basic starting point for a chord – if someone says, 'Play a C,' the chances are that they mean a root-position C.

Here's a root-position C chord:

Now, if we take away the bottom C note and put it on top of the chord, we leave E at the bottom of the chord. Because we've rearranged the positions of these notes from the root chord, we have created an *inversion*.

basic Keyboard Workout

It's still a C chord, it still has the same notes, but it's called a *first inversion*, as we have the next-lowest note, E, at the bottom of the chord, while the C is now at the top of chord, one octave higher than in the root-position chord.

If we take the E away from the bottom of the chord and leave G as our lowest note, we have created another, higher inversion – a second inversion. Check out the following notation:

Inversions can be created this way in any major or minor key. What does this mean for your playing? Well, very few pieces or parts use root-position chords from start to finish. (An exception can be found in early-'90s dance music.) Using different inversions gives much more contrast and dynamic interest to a piece and stops it from sounding stilted.

As an example, try playing the following chord sequence, which is all in root position:

Now play the same chords, but using the right-hand inversions below:

There's quite a difference, don't you agree? Notice how not every chord is inverted; instead, there's a mixture of root position and inversions.

However, because we're playing with both hands, the above examples illustrate only partial inversions in the right hand. To perform a full textbook inversion, the bottom note of the chord should change as well, and with two hands this means the bass (left-hand) note if playing solo or the bass line in a group context. As you can see from the previous example, the left-hand (bass) part stays on the root notes while the right hand plays different inversions. Therefore only partial inversions in the right hand, not full inversions, have actually been played, because the lowest note hasn't changed. When determining a chord's position – whether root position or inversion – it's always the bass (bottom) note that matters, whether playing with one hand, two hands or in a group with a separate bass line. This is where theory and practice often get muddled.

Most of the time, if you're reading a chord sheet it'll just say 'C, G,' and so on – it won't give details of inversions. In this instance, you can fairly safely assume that the bass notes will stay as root notes and the inversions that you play will be partial, confined to your right-hand parts, and it's up to you to decide whether or not to give them that extra colour and flavour.

If a chord chart asks your to play, for example, G major first inversion, it will almost certainly mean that the bass note is meant to come up to B. This doesn't mean that you necessarily have to play a first inversion with your right hand as well – judge what sounds better to you. Often, something like this would often be written as 'G/B' (often called *G over B*) instead, to avoid confusion.

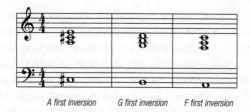

A first inversion   *G first inversion*   *F first inversion*

The right hand has stayed the same, but the bass part (left hand) has moved up to create first-inversion chords on the A, G and F. These are *full inversions*, distinctive in their sound. Often they seem as if they need to be resolved, as if waiting for another chord to be played.

So, how will you know when to use an inversion? Well, you'd usually have to deal with this if you were reading a chord chart, for instance (in which case you'd probably be confined to right-hand inversions, unless the music specifically directed otherwise), or writing your own music.

When playing along to a chord chart, listen to what the tune is doing. In this situation, you're accompanying the singer or instrumentalist, and your part should complement theirs, not override it. Often, chords and inversions that stay reasonably close to the tune, pitch-wise, work well.

For instance, look at the difference between the root-position and inversion examples above. The top notes of the root-position chords are all over the place. Imagine a tune being played or sung over that – it would sound a bit lumpy, to say the least. Now look at the example with inversions: the top notes of the chords stay within a much smaller area, and the part sounds smoother with it – much more suitable as a part.

I've written a simple tune with an accompanying chord chart. It has the same rhythmic feel as before. Try the chords in root position first, then experiment with a few inversions to hear and feel the differences in movement.

As a starting point when making up inversions, try to make the top notes of the chords stay reasonably close to the tune. For effect, of course, you can do anything you like – and I firmly believe in experimenting!

That sums up chords and inversions quite well. There's no substitute for getting used to the sound of them and then trying out new ideas. For example, look at well-known tunes from pop music songbooks (which have chord charts underneath) and try out the root positions and inversions of all the chords. The more you do of things like this, the larger the steps you'll be taking towards finding a sound – and approach – of your own.

8 INTERVALS

In a music context, the word *interval* refers to the distance between two notes, usually within an octave. Knowing what basic intervals are is indispensable – we need to know what intervals are, and what they sound like, before getting into looking at many more chords, as the names of the chords can refer to types of interval.

To help illustrate this, we'll look at our faithful C major scale. Counting the two Cs, one at the bottom and one at the top, we have eight notes. If I tell you that intervals can be called seconds, thirds, fourths, fifths, sixths, sevenths and octaves, you may well twig it straight away. For instance, if you want to know the interval (distance) between C and E, then count the notes: one, two, three – it's a third. Pretty simple. Likewise, the interval between E and A: one, two three, four – a fourth. It's important, though, to realise that an interval is the distance between *any* two notes, whether they're in the same key or not. I've used the C major scale here only because it's something easily written down and viewed.

minor2nd · major2nd · minor3rd · major3rd · perfect3rd · perfect5th

minor6th · major6th · minor7th · major7th · (octave)

Basic intervals

While C to E is indeed a third, it needs something else to give it a full description. As you know, within a scale, each note has to have a different letter name, which is why you have a B♭ rather than an A♯ in F major, and so on.

So, while the interval between C and E is a third, surely C to E♭ must also be a third? It is. We therefore need to have a separate terminology where this occurs, and indeed each of these thirds is known by a different name. C to E is a *major third*, whereas C to E♭ is a *minor third*. Listen to them both and you'll hear the difference.

Seconds, thirds, sixths and sevenths all have major and minor intervals. You can see that there's always one more semitone between notes of a major interval than between the notes of its minor version. Fourths and fifths are known as *perfect* intervals – because there's only one semitone between them, it's impossible to have major and minor versions.

More Tasty Chords...

The major and minor chords that we've looked at so far are invaluable. You'll use them a lot of the time in the forms we've covered to date. But they're also building blocks to be used as a base, a point from which to explore and find new variations. The more types of chords you know, the more colour and dynamics you can put into your music. Also, you won't have to make excuses when you come to tricky bars in a chord chart...

Major Sevenths

The major seventh is sometimes thought of (and rarely used because of it) as something of a jazz chord. I love jazz, and I love major-seventh chords, but I use the major seventh equally when playing pop or rock music, too. The principle behind it is very simple: its name tells you what you need to know – a major chord with a seventh on top. Let's take D, for example – play a D major triad, as below, and the seventh note of the major scale, which is C♯. That chord is now D major 7. Try this same procedure in other keys.

D major triad and major-seventh chord

Minor Sevenths

The minor seventh is a particularly useful chord and equally straightforward to work out. Let's find, for example, D minor 7. Play a D minor triad, as below, and add the seventh note of the (pure) minor scale. Again, try this in other minor keys.

D minor triad and minor-seventh chord

Straight Seventh Chords

As we're on D for the other examples, let's stay on it to illustrate this variety of seventh chord, which would usually be called simply *D7*. It's essentially a major chord, using the same triad just as the major seventh above, but it has a flattened seventh as the top note.

Straight seventh chords and their variations are often used in blues.

They're also often used to resolve chord sequences back to certain keys. For example, if a piece was in G major and the last chord was G, a D7 would be a typical chord to play before the G in order to resolve the sequence, like so:

D7–G major progression

Notice that the interval between those two chords, D to G, is a perfect fifth. Remember, it is the movement of the bass notes that tells you this. This progression is often known as a '5-1' (or, more usually, 'V-I'). In this instance, '1' means the G, or key note, and '5' the D, as it's a perfect fifth above.

Elevenths

The name for this chord is derived from the interval between the bottom and top notes of the chord. Elevenths were at one time thought of as classic 'disco' chords, particularly in ascending sequences. Taking G11 as an example, we obviously have G as our bottom note.

The rest of the chord is in the form of an F major triad, the last note of which is an 11th above the bass G.

You could obviously class this as F major over G – or F/G – and you'd be right. However, this could lead to inconsistencies, depending on which inversion of F you were playing, and it's this distinctive root-position F major chord with a top C – the 11th – that gives a G11, in this instance, the correct sound.

As a suggestion and a useful exercise for working out 11ths in other keys, find the 11th interval (an octave and a fourth, which is a perfect interval, so no major or minor versions) from the key note of the chord. This will be the top note of the major triad which forms the 11th chord.

Now, all of the chords I've shown you here are in their root, textbook forms. When reading lots of popular music or playing in a band, there will often be variations on how these appear. We've already seen with straight major and minor chords how inversions can make a lot of difference to the sound of the chord, particularly when playing along with a song, and of course you can invert all of the chords I've shown you here as well. Try changing their positions and exploring the changes in sound that result.

Also, when playing in a group of musicians, a guitarist's view of, say, Amaj7 would not be the version I showed you above. That's because he physically can't play the chord in that form, so he'll come up with a variation, which will essentially be that chord – maybe missing a note or two – and often inverting it slightly to make it possible to play. Be aware of this possibility when you come to find your own voicings.

9 RECOGNISING MUSIC BY EAR

Earlier on in the book, I said that being able to recognise chords and notes by ear is extremely important, and it certainly is. When we started to look at reading music from a stave, you were able to see what certain notes looked like on paper. That's actually quite helpful when ear training, because you start to get a mental image of which notes are higher or lower than others and what they sound like. A good start when recognising pitches of notes by ear is being able to find which area of the keyboard they belong to.

Identifying Intervals By Ear

To recognise notes by ear, familiarise yourself with the sounds of the intervals we've encountered already.

Play a C on your keyboard and, without playing any other notes, try to hum a C major scale. Then take another note, at random, and hum a major scale from there. It's not too difficult, is it? That's because your memory has formed a good image of it. If you can't hum the scale at first, keep trying and you'll manage it soon enough without too much bother. Play along on the keyboard to help until you can rely on your brain.

The ability to hum a major scale is extremely useful when it comes to recognising intervals. Some intervals are more easily recognised than others, and you may have a good enough sense of pitch to identify some without going through this process. With the more difficult ones, it can take a little longer, but if you keep training your ear, it will come.

Each interval has its own sound, obviously, but looking at intervals within an octave, as we are at the moment, they fall into distinct groups:

- Major and minor intervals (seconds, thirds, sixths and sevenths);

- Perfect intervals (4ths, 5ths and octaves).

Major And Minor Intervals

With the groups listed above, it helps to divide them again into two types: seconds and sevenths, and thirds and sixths.

- Thirds and sixths form parts of root-position and inverted major or minor chords. As such, they sound pleasantly harmonic and are used a lot when harmonising, for instance, or when you're finding a part to play or sing beneath a tune.

- Seconds and sevenths have a more distinctive, dissonant sound. A minor second is a semitone, and therefore the smallest interval you can have in the 12-tone scale we use in Western music. A major second is one semitone bigger; again you can hear the clash as it sounds, but with a slightly more tonal sound to it.

Sevenths can often be found at the tops of root-position chords, as we've seen, making them into major sevenths, minor sevenths and straight sevenths. However, when a seventh interval is played on its own, either major or minor, it can sound much more dissonant than when it's part of a chord. For example, try playing a G major seventh and a G minor seventh, and then take away the third and fifth. Hear how different both of the sevenths sound when you play them on their own.

Perfect Intervals

Perfect fourths and fifths have a clean, slightly 'spacey' sound. Taking the perfect fifth as an example, when this is played as part of a chord, such as a D major triad, this 'hollowness' is not as apparent. Remove the third to hear the fifth on its own, though, and you'll hear its characteristic sound.

Fifths are often used in left-hand parts because of their 'clean' sound. (We'll cover this more when we come to voicings of chords later on.)

Fourths have a similar, yet smaller, sound. To hear the interval within a chord, play a G major first inversion (D to G is a perfect fourth) and take away the B to hear the interval.

Try these exercises in different keys. Their varying colours can make the same intervals sound a little different until you're familiar with them.

Identifying Notes

Let's try a couple of experiments: on the CD, I'll play a note. Try to hum this note in your head. When you've done that, think what area of the keyboard it comes from. Is it high, low or in the middle? Again, when you think you've found the right area, try playing a few notes until you hit the same note as I've played on the CD. Repeat this a few times with the different notes I've given you.

Next, we're going to repeat this process, and afterwards I'll play another, higher note, which will be within the same major scale as the first one. Using the first, lower note as the tonic, hum up the scale until you reach the second note, then play the two notes together and see if you can hear and identify the interval.

Following this will be a series of notes which will be lower than the first, in a reverse of the above experiment.

To finish off, I'll play a series of intervals for you to identify. Don't panic if you can't recognise them by hearing their characteristics (and few people can until they've been doing it for a while) but work through the same technique – hum it, then find it and use a scale to work out which is the next note.

10 VOICINGS

In the previous chapter, we looked at how chords are basically comprised of a set of intervals, and how the sound of a chord changes when notes are removed, leaving certain intervals more exposed. With inversions, too, we've seen how the character of a chord can change when the notes are put in different positions. This reflects real-world playing well. All of the examples of chords and inversions we've encountered have been 'textbook' examples and, as I've said throughout the book, they are to be used as building blocks, a starting point for further exploration. In most circumstances, even when reading a piece, there will often be chord symbols written in above the notes. This is because a lot of the decisions regarding exactly which versions of a chord you should play are still down to you. To start to play effectively, we need to look a bit more carefully at how to voice chords – in other words, how to decide which notes and parts of chords to play, and which not to play...

Right- And Left-Hand Roles

Within the harmonic structure in a lot of popular music, both hands tend to have a fairly defined role. The right hand plays a tune and/or the principal chordal accompaniment; the left plays the bass plus other, more basic, chordal additions. There are exceptions, of course, but in the context of an accompaniment to a typical song, for instance, this is a common scenario. We therefore need to look at how to get each hand playing the kind of part that will sound right.

Let's take a typical triad – B minor. When played as shown in Example 1, over the page, it sounds light and clear but with a distinctly minor character. Move it down an octave (Example 2) and it has a deeper sound. Move it down another octave (Example 3), into the territory of left-hand playing, and it's starting to sound a little grotty. Down a further octave and it's decidedly unusable. This illustrates how the sounds of chords, and their voicings, change as we get lower down the keyboard.

As a basic rule of thumb, you need to listen carefully to how chords (such as that B minor triad) sound once you've gone down past the C an octave below middle C. This is where an appreciation of how intervals sound

Example 1: B minor root-position triad

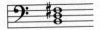

Example 2: B minor root-position triad an octave lower

Example 3: B minor root-position triad an octave lower

and work with each other makes a lot of difference. The lower you go, the more you'll find yourself taking out thirds and sixths, leaving fifths and, particularly, octaves. While this on its own would mean that the chord had no reference to a major or minor key (with no third present), the right hand will usually be filling in that kind of harmony.

When both hands play the B minor chord together –
the right hand playing a standard root-position triad
around the middle-C area of the keyboard – see how
the voicing of the left-hand chord changes the sound:

B minor triad (both hands)

B minor triad in right hand, fifth in left hand

You can hear distinctly the tighter, cleaner sound when
playing the perfect-fifth interval in the left hand.
Likewise, an octave in the left hand sounds similarly
uncluttered and powerful:

basic Keyboard Workout

B minor triad in right hand, octave B in left hand

You can see how interpretation of chords is a two-handed business, and sometimes you need to take steps in order to avoid over-cluttering the sound. For instance, the left hand, usually playing the bass, will often contain part of a chord that doesn't need to be replicated with the right. The chord shown in Example 4 is a textbook root-position Gmaj7, and yet when playing with both hands you would naturally put a G in the left hand as the bottom note underpinning the chord. Therefore, you could leave out the G at the bottom of the chord in the right hand, leaving the upper three notes (Example 5). The difference in sound between the two is subtle, but it's a good example of how small changes in voicings can make a difference. When playing with other instrumentalists in a group situation, it's very useful to remember this and to be aware that taking notes out of a chord creates a marked change in the way it sounds.

Example 4: G major-seventh chord

Example 5: G major-seventh chord without tonic

11 PEDALLING

On an acoustic piano there are two pedals built into the lower casing. The left one is known as a *soft pedal*, which in the case of an acoustic upright piano moves the hammers closer to the strings and in a grand piano moves them across so that they strike only two strings instead of three. Many electronic pianos have a similar arrangement and approximation of effect, which is to give a softer, more delicate tone.

Sustain Pedal

Most electric pianos should have a sustain pedal attached, and if this is the case you might already be familiar with what yours does. That might suggest it's only for certain types of players, and I do see a lot of synth players who don't use one. Whether you've considered using one or not, I think it's one of the essential things to get to grips with and use properly, whatever style of music you play. Sloppy use of the sustain pedal sounds messy, but when used effectively it can be one of the main tools to benefit and polish your playing.

If your keyboard hasn't got a sustain pedal built in, the chances are it will have a socket at the back to accept one. It should be in the form of a normal quarter-inch jack socket, into which you plug the lead end of a separate pedal. These are readily available from most music shops and can be very cheap, although not always shaped like a piano's. However, as long as you can get a reliable feel on it and it doesn't slide around when depressed, that shouldn't matter very much.

So, when to use it? Well, let's try an experiment with the pedal attached and working. Press it down and hold while you play several notes at random. As its name implies, it will now sustain all the notes you play until it's released. Its most common use is to enable you to move from one chord to another with maximum smoothness. It can also be used for effect, as in our experiment, although this highlights one of the dangers of using the sustain pedal – it can easily be used in the wrong place and make a real mess of the sound.

As a rule of thumb, whenever it's needed, the pedal should be reapplied whenever the chord changes. Holding it down while you play two or more chords in different keys will sometimes cause dissonance, but if the same basic chord is held for a few bars holding it down can be effective. Care should be taken not to overuse it, though.

With chords, it's easier to grasp its usefulness, because when playing a chord with any number of fingers in either hand, when you have to move to another chord even a short distance away there will inevitably be a gap as you take your hands off the keyboard to play the next chord. With a sustain pedal, this isn't a problem. Depress the pedal while playing the first chord, holding the sound on. You're then free to take your hands off the keyboard and position them to play the next chord while the first chord is still sounding. Then release the pedal as you play the second chord. If done properly, the transition will be smooth and seamless.

To illustrate this, here's a quick example. Play one bar of an E major chord and one bar of A major, without pedal first:

You can hear the gap during the change between the two chords, and it sounds a little awkward, so we'll depress the sustain pedal as we play the first chord. Now, moving our hands up to the A major, we can play the chord while releasing the pedal.

The important bit is the release of the pedal. If this is done too early, there'll still be a gap; too late and the two chords will blur together in an unpleasant way. The secret is to bring the pedal up at the same time as playing the next chord so that it becomes a simultaneous motion. At first it can seem strange doing this, as if you've left it too late, but with familiarity it will become second nature.

When the part in question has a bit more rhythmic activity to it than the previous example, the pedal can still be used. Imagine a typical pop-rock ballad, with the keyboard part playing a fours-type crotchet rhythm, such as that shown below:

basic Keyboard Workout

Because the keyboard part is playing the same chord throughout each bar, the pedal can again be reapplied at the end of the first bar. As you're playing a chord on the last beat of the bar, however, be aware that there's far less time at the end of the bar to move your hand to the next chord. Repeat and go around the chord change a few times.

That's the basis of pedalling. With practice, it can be used during very subtle and rhythmically complex pieces of music. Once you've mastered the feel of it through playing simple parts, you'll find your technique with it growing as you develop your overall playing ability. Remember that pedalling is something that a listener should be largely unaware of, so use it accordingly.

You might find markings on pieces of music indicating where the use of the sustain pedal is required: underneath the bottom stave, a horizontal line will be drawn with two small vertical lines at each end to signify where it should be applied and released. Usually it will have a small 'ped' sign before it. However, unless you're playing pieces with dedicated piano parts, it's unlikely you will see this sign very often.

12 DYNAMICS

When music is created and performed, its purpose is to interest and inspire the listener, to create moods and colours, excitement and darkness. Music does this in many different ways, some of which we've looked at already, such as the different sounds of major and minor chords and the ways in which inversions can make chords of the same key change in character. Yet the main ingredient in making music really mean something is within the way it's played. Two different performers can make the same piece of music sound and feel completely different by use of dynamics.

The term *dynamics* means different things. To illustrate this at one end of the spectrum, think of a completely undynamic noise, such as a cheap electric alarm clock going off, making a monotonous single tone. Although the alarm has a pitch and is technically playing a note, it is not music, merely noise. And yet, when playing that same note on a keyboard, merely changing the way in which it's played can make it sound totally different.

basic Keyboard Workout

This illustrates that there is rather more to music than just playing notes. It's the *feel*, the human element, that makes music tell a story and reach people. Otherwise, it would be nothing but a series of mechanical noises.

Out of all the indications of dynamic change on a piece of music, the most recognisable and easily understandable are known as *dynamic markings*. These are most commonly found in pieces of classical music, and are formally known by Italian names such as *forte* (marked *f*) and *piano* (marked *p*). Put simply, they mean *loud* and *soft*, respectively.

Think when you listen to music. The degrees of loudness and softness are varying all the time. They can be heard changing within a bar or a beat, or a section of music can change in dynamic over a long period, gathering energy or diminishing to nothing.

Starting on page 98 you'll find a straightforward 4/4 backing track (I've titled it 'Released'), a typical pop/rock ballad accompaniment. It's typified by the right-hand part playing a chord on every beat of the bar. Played without any dynamics at all, it sounds pretty awful and dull, and yet, with some thought and feel, it can sound completely different. To help apply this process, look at the basic information the piece gives you at the start. The tempo is the first indication – a slow piece will need a different approach from a fast one. The time signature is another – is it in simple or compound time?

Look at the key signature. Even if a piece is in a minor key, this doesn't necessarily mean it is slow and dull, any more than a major key has to reflect brightness. Instead, it's the movement of chords during the piece that gives it character and reference, as well as the types of chord used. So look at the chords that run through the piece and their duration. While this part is a fairly simple one that keeps a relatively steady movement of chords throughout, I'll illustrate how the feel of the piece changes very subtly, but importantly, within a few beats at a time.

Notice the lines that run above the music at the start of the piece for four bars at a time – these indicate the length of a particular phrase. Imagine talking for a couple of minutes at a time – you'd have to stop and take breath, wouldn't you? Phrasing markings can be interpreted in a similar manner – imagine them as guiding you to the length of a statement, after which you take an almost imperceptible breath. It's more felt than heard, but it's another important factor that helps music come alive.

'Released'

Many songs and instrumental tracks like this run around a four-bar, 16-beat structure. It's one of the 'natural'-feeling durations within music that is used a lot. Dance tracks, on which parts are often brought in and out to give dynamics and inject excitement, commonly work around structures in groups of four – four bars doing one thing, something else brought in or taken out after another four, and so on. It's a formula that feels very comfortable within the human body rhythm. This part conforms to this structure. Within the first four bars, the feel of the music can be heard to ebb and flow.

You can hear an emphasis on the first beat of bars 1 and 3. In a way, this is because it's answering the 'question' that is being asked during bar 2. The move to the minor chord in that bar changes the bright, sunny feel of bar 1, and it's almost as if it's asking the question, 'Where are we going?' The answer to this question is, back to the major chord at the start of bar 3 and the reaffirmation of the initial, brighter feeling. This happens again several times, and it's one of the many subtle variations within the piece that give it meaning.

The dynamic marking at the start of the piece is *mezzo forte*, marked *mf* (moderately loud).

And then, after eight bars, the piece moves onto another section, a bridge. *Bridge* is a term used somewhat loosely – a bridge is not of a pre-determined length and can occur anywhere in a piece. The term is commonly used to refer to a section of music that changes slightly from what has come before and either directs it to a chorus (in a typical song format) or reinstates the previous section (as in this case). Here, the bridge has a similar major-to-minor progression as the opening eight-bar section, yet the alteration of chords give it a feeling of change, another uncertainty. The dynamic markings change to reflect this, although not straight away. The term *dim* (*diminuendo*) tells you to quieten down gradually, so where this appears at the start of bar 14, bring the volume down until the next dynamic marking, *mezzo piano* – marked *mp* (moderately quiet) – indicates that you've reached the required level.

The phrasing in the bridge reflects the change in the piece. Instead of occurring every four bars, the phrasing rises and falls over the first two bars (13 and 14), then each of the last two bars (15 and 16) is phrased separately. This gives a distinct feeling of a tiny pause for breath before bar 16, as if the music is gathering itself up to make a statement.

As the opening section is reinstated at bar 17, there's a natural feeling of release and energy. Because of this, the overall dynamic level of the piece changes in the last two bars of the bridge – *cresc* (*crescsendo*) means getting gradually louder – and over those final two bars of the bridge the level grows from *mp* to *f*.

Over the last two bars of the piece, a feeling of *rallentando* (getting slower, usually abbreviated as '*rall*') occurs. Think about it – most tracks that end with a dead stop, such as this one, don't just get to the end and stop with an abrupt halt. Instead the music wants to 'introduce' the end by easing back a bit. It makes the listener aware that the end of the piece has been reached.

So, although this is essentially a pretty straightforward progression of chords, it now sounds like a piece of music. It involves you, and the listener, to a degree that wouldn't have happened had you just played through the chords. Music must be more than a procession of notes and instructions – look into the music for the ebbs and flows, for the sometimes 'hidden' bits and colours that can be brought out.

13 TECHNIQUE AND MUSICALITY

You might be asking why we're spending more time on technique when it's a subject we covered earlier. The fact is that improving your technique is a never-ending journey. A lot of the fundamentals – such as posture and basic hand position – might have been covered, but to move on you must use these techniques described in the first book as building blocks with which to develop the skills you need to get more out of music.

Earlier in the book, I explained a few things that might have surprised you, such as the fact that there's a lot more to having a good technique than just being able to rattle off a few quick runs. Instead, it's *how* you do something that counts, and in time we're going to find out more about what that really means.

Technique is basically your body's ability to do what your mind tells it. One of the things a good technique gives you is an ability to do this while keeping a *form* – a good physical relationship with your instrument that allows you to play to your maximum ability. This doesn't necessarily mean performing impressive-sounding, very technical bits of music; more importantly, it's about physically being able to put your own musical ideas into your playing.

Technical And Musical Playing

Music isn't just a succession of notes. In songs or tracks you know and love, dynamics and feel make them come alive and mean something. When you're playing yourself, you can often feel the need to make more of these musical highs and lows. To do this effectively, you need to know both how to do it musically (ie what to do and when to do it) and how to make it happen physically. This is a good example of how technique and musicality are linked together – without the technique to help you play what's in your mind, you'll never be able to do it.

So, first of all you need to acquire the technique and ability to start putting these things – dynamics, feel and phrasing – into your playing. The first thing we'll look at is the use of arm weight.

Arm Weight

To start with, make sure your hand is kept in an arched position with the fingers bent, keeping your wrist relaxed – ie free to move up and down.

Now, someone asks you to play a powerful C major chord straight away. What happens? Chances are, your arms lift up, with the wrist held rigid, and you plonk down your hands on the keyboard as hard as you can. While the sound is probably loud, it will also be hard and won't feel good to play. It's hard to imagine being able to put a lot of feel into music while playing like that.

Now try the other extreme. Play that same C major chord, this time as quietly as you can. If you still keep your wrist rigid, the chord *might* sound OK, but if you then try the same action several times you'll probably end up with some of the notes sounding uneven or – worse than that – inconsistent.

What I'm getting at here is the idea that keeping the wrist free to move up and down is the key to moving on with not only your technique but also your playing in general. If you fall into the habit of keeping the wrist rigid, you'll never really develop your abilities to anything like their full extent.

Let's try the loud chord again. This time, we're still going to produce a powerful sound, but in a different way – using the weight of the arm. Instead of just lifting your arms up all as one, first of all find and feel the notes you're going to play while the hand is resting on the keyboard.

basic Keyboard Workout

Lift your wrist up and forward slightly, exerting a small amount of pressure on your fingers to lift them off the keyboard and raise your arm up. Your wrist will now be the highest point on the arm. With the arm still in the air, bring the hand up so that the wrist falls down to a lower point. Now combine the two feelings of just letting the weight of the arm fall down to its usual position and the wrist pivoting forward to allow the fingers to play the chord.

As the hand makes contact with the keyboard, the wrist should be back to its normal position, parallel to the floor. Don't exaggerate and let it sink any lower, and make sure your fingers are bent at the ends.

Try this exercise a few times. You'll feel that, if you allow the weight of your arm to descend on the chord, you can produce a more powerful yet still sweet-sounding chord. It can be difficult to achieve accuracy initially, so don't worry about a few wrong notes at the moment. It's the feeling we're after at this stage.

Now the quiet version. Apply the same principle but this time, when you come down to play the chord, you'll become aware that the speed at which you bring the wrist and arm down has an important bearing on how it sounds. Do this very slowly and you'll develop the ability not only to play a very subtle chord or note extremely quietly, but you should also notice that something is different. You can now *feel*, and anticipate, how the chord will sound before it's played; you can mould the sound in your mind.

Now, of course you're not necessarily going to be able to play this way all the time – the occasions when you have the opportunity to place a single note like this are limited – but what these exercises *do* show you is:

1   How your wrist needs to be flexible and relaxed in order to help you get much more expression;

2   How to visualise and anticipate the way in which notes will sound before you play them.

This is a very condensed explanation of the topic of arm weight. Like everything else, you need to spend some time practising before you become comfortable and familiar with it.

The reason why I've covered the subject at this stage of the book is because I want you to integrate the concept of feel, and touch, into everything you play. When you play exercises such as scales and arpeggios, which can sometimes seem repetitive and boring, you want the time spent doing them to be as useful as possible when you come to play tracks or pieces. Therefore, there's no point in doing exercises mindlessly, just hammering up and down the keyboard; you need to *play* them every time you do them. There are a number of ways you can do this – for instance, practise getting louder and then quieter within the ascending and descending parts of the exercise.

Getting To Grips With Arm Weight

The following exercise is useful as a warm-up every time you play. As you can see, it features a major and minor chord followed by an inverted major chord from a different key to step up to the next chord. Use the technique described above to play each chord. As with all exercises, the slower you do them, the more progress you'll make. If it feels awkward for a little while, just stay with it, as your muscles will soon learn and adapt. Pedal between each chord to make the transition as smooth as possible.

This is also pretty good practice for recognising accidentals. As the exercise is in no set key, there's no point in having a dedicated key signature. Therefore, bear in mind the primary rules about how you read accidentals, as explained after the notation.

Play slowly, using the sustain pedal on each chord

OK then, accidentals. Normally, in a piece which has a specified key signature at the start – for instance, G major and its key signature of F♯ – wherever an F♯ occurs within that piece, it won't need a sharp sign before it to remind you. Any F you see – unless it had another accidental sign (♮ or ♭) before it – should automatically be played as F♯, because it's in the key signature.

In an exercise like this, however, where there is no key signature – all accidentals are written in place – any note that has an accidental before it should be played in that altered state (ie with the accidental) if it crops up again within the same bar. If it *is* to be changed, it will have to be indicated by either a natural, sharp or flat sign.

Where there are lots of chord changes in a short space of time, as in this exercise, it can take some remembering before you get comfortable with this.

14 **DEXTERITY**

While I might have given the impression that dexterity (ie being able to play quickly and accurately) is secondary in importance to feel, they should be considered as being intrinsically related – just like most things in music. The techniques you need to master in order to improve your touch – such as arm weight and a flexible wrist – are also essential requirements for developing dexterity, but, like all things, we can't begin at the end; we have to build this ability up in stages.

Get your form right – that's one of the things you really have to make sure of, because if you rush and fail to get your basework right, progress will be slow. I've known some promising players who, because they couldn't be bothered to play anything through slowly, were sadly still at the same stage, scrabbling along, a couple of years later. And dexterity is the same: you can't rush it, even though your goal is to improve the clarity and speed of your playing.

As I mentioned in the 'Arm Weight' section of the

previous chapter, in order to play to your maximum ability, flexibility is necessary, particularly in the wrist. Put your hands on the keyboard, ready to play a C major scale. Think about the feeling you had when you played the previous chordal exercise – your wrist was flexible and relaxed. Now, you need to keep that feeling in mind, but as you're going to play a straightforward scale, you don't need to use any movement in the wrist; keep it as flexible and relaxed as possible while still holding it parallel to the floor, and make good use of the fingers.

Play (slowly!) a scale that you feel comfortable with, keeping the wrist flexible but the hand as steady as possible, using just the fingers to play the notes. Try to lift them a bit more than usual, and get to the bottom of each note when you play it. Repeat this – again, slowly – a few times and your fingers may feel as though they've had a bit of a workout. The upper forearm may also ache a bit. That's OK, although be careful not to overdo it.

IMPORTANT: You mustn't feel any aching or discomfort underneath the forearm, in the area where you would buckle a watch. If you do, you're overdoing it and you need to stop and have a rest.

Keep doing this exercise slowly – don't be tempted to rush through. My recommendation would be to start your practice session by playing the arm-weight chord exercise for a few minutes and then run through a few scales, as described above. When building up technique like this, the 'little and often' mode of practising really works, so instead of plodding through exercises for half an hour, you'd be better off doing three ten-minute spells during the day instead.

Practising Different Rhythms

After a couple of weeks engaged in the exercises described above, you should start to feel meaningful benefits. Your fingers should have acquired a bit of extra strength and your general playing should feel a little easier. The next step is to introduce different rhythms into the exercises to even them out.

This is an area of considerable benefit because, as you're aware, certain fingers have less strength than others. It's easy enough to lift your second finger up and down on its own, but try it with the fourth or fifth finger and it can be a lot harder. Practising different rhythms helps to even out slight but noticeable flaws in timing, particularly when using the weaker fingers.

Firstly, using the C major scale as a reference point, try it like this:

Immediately afterwards, try it like this:

It's important that you play the second pattern straight after the first one; don't do just one pattern on its own. Again, play this exercise through a few times, first one pattern and then the other.

Next, using a slightly longer version of the scale, try it in triplets, giving the start of each group of three notes a definite accent. (The number 3 over the first note in each triplet group is a well-used sign indicating a triplet figure.)

Finish off by playing normally. You'll be surprised at how different this feels after playing in different rhythms.

This technique of practising in rhythms is always useful. Don't restrict it to scales and arpeggios, either; use it whenever you have a difficult passage to play – perhaps a tricky solo. It really does work!

I've used the scale of C major here as an example, but you'd be advised to try the same idea with all the other scales and arpeggios you know at this stage. We're about to learn a few new chords, so incorporate these as well into your practising. I'll suggest particularly useful examples as we go along.

15 MORE HARMONIC KNOWLEDGE

Augmented And Diminished Harmonies

In addition to major and minor harmonies, there are other commonly used variations that are essential to know. Many players use augmented and diminished intervals and chords without realising it and yet would struggle to explain them if asked. They're nothing to be scared of, though, and here I'll illustrate exactly what they are and how they can be used.

Notice that I've used the word *harmonies* to describe them. That's because the tones that make up these augmented and diminished variations are more than just different versions of an interval, scale or chord; they come together to form harmonic colours and a distinctive musical sound.

The Augmented Fourth/ Diminished Fifth

Let's recap slightly to help you understand the basic concept of these terms. Back in *Part 1*, we looked at how all chords were basically comprised of a set of intervals. Here's a rundown of most of intervals to be found within an octave:

Looking carefully at the above illustration, you might notice that there's one interval not covered. There's a perfect fourth and a perfect fifth, but between those two intervals lies another note – in this example, the black note between F and G. Welcome to an extremely interesting new harmony...

It initially looks rather confusing, but for simple reasons this new interval can be called either an augmented fourth or a diminished fifth. A quick rule of thumb: for augmented, think bigger; for diminished, think smaller. That's one reason why what is essentially the same interval can be known by two different names.

But surely this is a bit of a palaver, you may ask. Isn't this a prime example of musical rudiments getting up its own backside? Well, maybe, but the main reason for it is so that it can accommodate the intervals within different key structures. For instance, if you were playing a piece in the key of D major, which has F♯ as part of its key signature, you would write, and classify, that interval as C–F♯ – therefore an augmented fourth. Meanwhile, in the key of D♭ major – which has no sharps in its key signature but five flats, including G♭ – you would regard the interval as C–G♭, a diminished fifth. This distinction might seem like something you really don't need to be bothered with, but as you start to encounter these intervals in different sharp- and flat-based keys, you'll appreciate how the way you think of them affects the way you play.

Augmented 4th in D7 chord

Diminished 5th in G♭7 chord

Putting Them Into Practice

Of course, these two intervals sound the same, so despite what I said above, many people refer to this interval only as a *flattened fifth*. At least you know the reasons behind the two variations now. I'll refer to them as aug4 and dim5 from now on. For now, though, let's have a look at the ways in which they're used musically. Play the two notes of the interval one after the other, like this...

...and you can hear it has a very distinctive sound. It was actually at one time (many centuries ago) thought of as something of an evil interval, and was branded by the Church the *Diabolus in musica*, an unholy combination of notes that, it was feared, would summon the horned one himself. It can certainly suggest a dark image, particularly when played lower down in pitch, and it's a beloved tool of umpteen classic rock tracks – for example Jimi Hendrix's 'Purple Haze' starts off with an E and B♭ played together, and you can hear the interval used regularly on many contemporary songs, particularly on the darker, goth-like rock numbers.

A characteristic of the interval is that it sounds like it needs to be resolved. The tension it creates can be eased by moving to a perfect fifth to give this sound:

Resolving an aug4/dim5 interval to a perfect fifth

For an effective example of this, listen to the Led Zeppelin track 'Kashmir' (the original or the Puff Daddy remix) and 'Wake Up' by Rage Against The Machine (the start of the track, which is used during the end titles in *The Matrix*). You can really hear how the very simple change between the opening aug4/dim5 to the subsequent perfect fifth works.

Played As Part Of A Chord
Like most other intervals that have a distinctive sound when played on their own, when used as part of a chord the sound of the aug4/dim5 can be very different. For example, when it's less exposed, the interval can easily lose its 'dark' quality:

Augmented fourth (C–F♯ in the right hand) within a D7 chord

You can still hear the interval within this chord, but it's taken on a very different character. This reinforces the meaning behind the second paragraph in this chapter – don't think of these combinations of notes as being merely intervals; think of them as harmonic colours, as much as anything else, that can change depending upon their context.

Augmented And Diminished Chords And Arpeggios

So far, the chords and arpeggios we've encountered have been either major or minor. However, each key also has its own augmented and diminished version. Like the aug4/dim5 interval, these intervals have a distinctive sound and are commonly used in certain musical situations.

Augmented Chord

We'll use C major again as a starting point for an example. A standard C major triad looks like this:

To make a C augmented triad, we simply sharpen the top note (G) by one semitone to G♯:

If you look carefully at this augmented triad, you'll see that it's composed of two major-third intervals: C–E and E–G♯. Wherever you are on the keyboard, if you want to build a root augmented chord, just measure two major thirds above the note you're playing. For instance, in the key of D, a major third above the root is F♯ and a major third above F♯ is A♯. Presto! There's your root-position D augmented triad.

You can form an arpeggio of an augmented triad in exactly the same way as with a major or minor. Using the C augmented triad as described earlier, simply add another major third – a top C – to the top of the octave and play it ascending and descending:

C augmented arpeggio and chord

Diminished Chord

Remember what I said about the general rule for augmented and diminished harmonies? For augmented, think bigger; for diminished, think smaller. To form a diminished chord from the standard C major triad, flatten the E and G by one semitone to make E♭ (D♯) and G♭ (F♯) respectively:

C diminished arpeggio and chord

Comparing this with the augmented triad – which was comprised of *major* thirds in sequence – you can see that the diminished version is made up from *minor* thirds. You can use this general rule of thumb to find root-position diminished triads anywhere on the keyboard.

However, the way in which a diminished chord or arpeggio is constructed throws up an interesting question. The augmented chord was completed by just sticking another major third above the augmented triad, which brought us back to the keynote (C in the example). However, as a diminished chord is formed from a series of minor thirds, adding another minor third to the top of the triad brings you to A, while another minor third above that will bring you to the keynote (C again in this example).

Therefore an augmented chord is made up of four notes, whereas a diminished chord is made up of five.

Inverted Examples

In just the same way as normal major and minor chords have root-position and inverted variations, so do augmented and diminished chords. Likewise, inverted versions are useful for exactly the same reasons: to give a sequence of chords more colour or contrast and to give you more choice when trying to find a part that fits in a group or recording scenario.

Inverted Augmented Chord

If you want to invert either an augmented or diminished chord, follow the same principle as with a major or minor.

Let's take C augmented (in its root position) as our first example. We know it's in root position because C is at the bottom of the chord. To find the first inversion, remove the C to make the next highest note, E, the new bottom note. The C is then placed at the top of the triad to make this:

C augmented triad (first inversion)

The procedure for finding the second inversion is equally simple – the G♯ is put at the bottom of the chord and the C and E at the top. (Note that all these variations of the augmented chord, root position and inversions, are still heard as of a series of major thirds.)

C augmented triad (second inversion)

Inverted Diminished Chord

Using C diminished (in root position) as our reference, and following the same procedure, it's pretty simple to find the first and second inversions. To make a first inversion, put the E flat at the bottom of the chord and the other three notes arranged as follows:

C diminished triad (first inversion)

Similarly, in the second inversion, the G♭ goes to the bottom of the chord and the A, C and E♭ go above. With a diminished chord, it's also possible to have a third inversion, with the A beneath and the C, E♭ and G♭ on top.

C diminished triad (second inversion)

It's very easy to make arpeggios out of all of these inversions, whether augmented or diminished. In addition, take the time to use this bit of knowledge I've given you to discover these new harmonies in different keys; it won't take long and will help greatly in developing your musical ear.

16 FURTHER SCALES

Harmonic And Melodic Minor Scales

We've already looked at basic major and minor harmonies, enough to know that the main difference between the two centres on the third note of the scale. The flattened (semitone lower) third of the minor gives it a naturally darker, discernibly different sound from a major scale.

The first version of the minor scale we looked at was the pure minor scale, but there are two more versions of the minor scale that you need to know: the *harmonic* and the *melodic*. Both of these new versions still have a flattened third note, giving them the classic minor characteristic; the main difference between the harmonic and melodic is the fact that the harmonic scale uses the same notes both ascending and descending (ie going up and down), whereas the melodic follows one pattern going up and another coming down. While you might not see the point of learning another couple of versions of a scale, remember that scales and arpeggios are tools that you'll be using all the time in your playing, so the more progress you make here, the more you'll appreciate that both of these types of minor scale are really useful to know, particularly when you come to play solos and lead lines. They also each have a distinctive sound, which helps to get your ear used to recognising certain types of intervals.

Harmonic Minor Scale

Written out below for comparison is a pure A minor scale and then an A harmonic minor scale.

Pure A minor scale

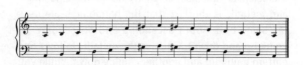

A harmonic minor scale

The two are very similar – the harmonic differs when we come to the seventh note of the scale, which is sharpened a semitone higher than it appears in the pure minor. You can easily recognise the sound of a harmonic minor from the interval between the sixth and seventh notes, which gives it an almost Arabic flavour.

Key Signature

Referring to the relationship between major and minor scales, we know that A minor's relative key is C major and that C major has no sharps or flats. In this harmonic minor, however, we have introduced a G♯, so how can the two share the same key signature? Well, it's taken as a characteristic of a minor scale that the seventh note is raised (sharpened) so that it's not included in the key signature. Therefore, C major and A minor share the same key signature, and similarly all relative majors and minors share the same key signature.

Melodic Minor Scale

You'll hear many a widdly guitarist practising his melodic minors – as I said, one of the scale's more direct uses is as an element of many solos. It can seem conceptually a little strange at first to have a scale that's different ascending and descending, but that's actually one of the most useful things about it, as we'll see.

A melodic minor scale

I've used A minor again as an example here. The first five notes of the melodic scale are identical to those in its harmonic counterpart, but after that things get a bit more interesting. On the way up, the sixth note is sharpened to F♯. A melodic-minor scale keeps the sharpened seventh already present in the harmonic minor, making the last four notes of the ascending scale identical to those in A major. On the way down, both of these notes – the sixth and seventh – are flattened (taken down a semitone) to make a pure A minor scale.

So the melodic minor is something of a hybrid, using elements of the harmonic minor, the pure minor and the major. This is why it's such a well-used musical tool, because it reflects real-world playing. Most parts and pieces of music use a selection of major and minor chords; you rarely find anything that uses only one type all the way through. Therefore – particularly when it comes to soloing – you need to have tools in your box like these scales (and to have a trained ear) in order to recognise and be able to play over different chord changes. Soloing, and improvising in general, is something that can put fear into some players, yet this is often because they've never learned the basics – such as scales like these – that would help them do it. (We'll cover the topic of improvisation in a later chapter, but putting in the bit of effort required to learn these scales in as many keys as possible before then will help you no end.)

Pentatonic And Whole-Tone Scales

Now we're really moving into the area where we'll be starting to use scales and similar tools within playing. You're not very likely to play music using complete ascending and descending types of scale; instead you'll find that familiarity allows you to take parts of them and then use and adapt them to the musical situation you're in. Most importantly, as you learn these new scales, you're also training your ear to listen and recognise their sound. Later on in the book, I'll be asking you to play pieces with backing tracks that will illustrate how some of these new tools can be used.

Pentatonic Scale

The pentatonic scale is very widespread throughout all kinds of music and is the basis of many tunes from all over the world. Its name gives some idea of its make-up: the word *penta* means 'five' in Greek and, reflecting this, the scale has only five different notes within the octave, as opposed to the seven that appear in regular majors and minors.

C pentatonic scale

The pentatonic scale differs from the major scale by leaving out the fourth and seventh notes. The result is a clean-sounding succession of notes that harmonically have a very sweet sound. Like all scales, the pentatonic scale can be particularly widely used as a basis for ideas and soloing, yet understanding it can also be invaluable when it comes to constructing different versions of chords. For example, try playing all of the notes in the scale above together, as you would a chord. Without the presence of the fourth and seventh, it's quite a pleasant-sounding chord. That's because most of the notes left remaining are part of either the major chord (in this case C) or its relative minor chord (A minor).

Whole-Tone Scale

As its name implies, each step of this scale is a tone apart from its neighbour, therefore allowing only six different notes within the octave. Historically, while also appearing in earlier music, the whole-tone scale became widely used in the late 19th and early 20th centuries within a Gallic-based style of music known as *Impressionism*. One of the fundamental characteristics of this style was the use of music to suggest certain images; pieces often would be given a name which the music would be written to suggest. Composers within the Impressionist movement, such as Debussy and Ravel, made much use of the whole-tone scale. Play it through and you'll hear its mysterious, rather beautiful quality.

C whole-tone scale

Blues Scale

Blues is of course a musical genre in its own right and is the basis for much modern pop music, yet its harmonic characteristics are so commonly found, in all types of music, that it's essential to look at the basic blues scale in this chapter.

The scale is composed of the root (in this case C), flattened third, fourth, augmented fourth, fifth and

C blues scale

flattened seventh. Individual notes from the blues scale, such as the flattened third and the flattened seventh, can give any melody within any style of music a bluesy feel. Play a C7 chord in your left hand and, while holding it down, use your right hand to play the blues scale above. You'll hear what I mean about those two notes in particular.

All of the examples in this section are in C for illustrative purposes. Just as before, though, I'd urge you to take the time to explore all the scales in different keys. Get used to the different sounds and colours that this introduces. Tackle them in just a few keys at a time – don't rush into it. You might well find that a scale book – available from most music shops – will come in helpful here; it will give you all of the types of scale we've covered here, with fingering as well.

17 SUS4 AND NINTH CHORDS

A couple more chord types you'll encounter on a regular basis are suspended fourths (usually abbreviated to *sus4s*) and major and minor ninths.

We'll start with the suspended-fourth triad and chord first. It's very similar to a major triad, but the name of the chord gives you a good clue as to its real identity. Compared to a major – which is composed of the first, third and fifth notes of the major scale – the sus4 uses the first, fourth and fifth:

Csus4 triad

As with any other root-position triad, you can add the key note at the top of the octave to get a fuller sound:

Csus4 chord

Very often a sus4 chord will resolve to a major or minor immediately afterwards. Try playing a C major or C minor chord after a sus4 chord, as shown below:

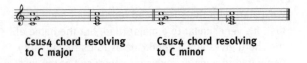

Csus4 chord resolving to C major   **Csus4 chord resolving to C minor**

The sus4 is often used when a major would sound a little too bright. It has a solid but thoughtful quality. Like any other chord, a sus4 can also be inverted, or notes can be taken out to make it sound better in a part.

Major And Minor Ninths

We've looked at major and minor sevenths already. Once you've understood what they are, it's only a small leap to take ninths on board. To refresh your memory, the 7 in a major- or minor-seventh chord means that the top note of the chord is a seventh above the root-position note. Hence a Cmaj7 looks like this...

Cmaj7 chord

...and a Cmin7 looks like this:

Cmin7 chord

A ninth uses either a major or minor seventh as its base (depending on which version you need to play) and includes a ninth on top as well. In this chord, however, the ninth is always a major interval (or an octave and a major second, if you prefer) above the root note whether the chord is major or minor. So a Cmaj9 chord is composed of a Cmaj7 chord with a major ninth on top and a Cmin9 chord is made up of a Cmin7 chord but also with a major ninth on top, as shown below. So you can see that, in both instances here, the top note is D:

139

basic Keyboard Workout

Just to show you another example, take Emaj9 and Emin9. An Emaj7 chord is this:

Emaj7 chord

To find the major-ninth chord, simply put a major ninth (an octave and a major second) above E, which in this case is F#, as shown here:

Likewise, to play Emin9, find an Emin7 and, again, put a major ninth (F#) above E.

18 MORE ABOUT RHYTHM

More About Compound Time

The only compound time signature covered so far is 6/8, while the other most commonly used variations are 3/8, 9/8 and 12/8. They're all very simple to get your head around because they all follow the same basic premise of compound time: that each bar is made up of quaver-length beats, in groups of three.

So, to recap on 6/8, we know that the first figure, 6, refers to the number of beats in a bar. The second figure, 8, refers to the length of each beat – ie eighth notes, also known as quavers. The characteristic of compound time – that the beats are joined together in groups of three – makes a 6/8 bar look like this:

The procedure for understanding 3/8, 9/8 and 12/8 time signatures is exactly the same. For instance, 3/8 means that there are three eighth-note beats in a bar...

...9/8 means there are nine eighth-note beats in a bar...

...and 12/8 means – you guessed it – 12 eighth-note beats in a bar:

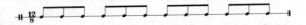

When you hear these rhythms being played, they all have a very distinctive sound because of the way the three beats are grouped together. It's natural to put a slight accent on the first of each group of three, which in turn can lead to regarding each group of three as one beat. Therefore you can often feel that 6/8 has a two-in-the-bar feel, 9/8 a three-in-the-bar feel and 12/8 a four-in-the-bar feel. If you're not sure whether the piece of music you're listening to is in simple time (eg 4/4) or compound time (eg 12/8), just listen for the difference in feel between the two.

Notating Rhythms In Compound Time

When reading music in compound time, certain note values are used to emphasise that grouping of three eighth-note beats. We've seen how three beats played in succession are written down, but when writing quarter and eighth notes (and rests) individually there is a certain pattern to observe.

The grouping together of three eighth notes leads naturally to a much-used rhythmic pattern of quarter-note/eighth-note or the reverse, eighth-note/quarter-note, as shown below. (The way that these patterns actually sound gives compound time one of its main characteristics.) Rests are written in a similar manner, with the quarter-note/eighth-note pattern (or reverse) commonly used. Remember that, although compound time is often felt in two, three or four, depending on the time signature (6/8, 9/8 or 12/8), the pulse of three quavers per beat always runs throughout.

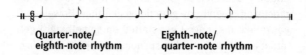

**Quarter-note/
eighth-note rhythm**

**Eighth-note/
quarter-note rhythm**

19 PRACTISING

Practising – the very word brings a groan to some people. As a youngster, I would often loathe practising because I had to put in a certain amount of effort to keep up lessons. For a child, it can seem to be monotonous and boring. When you add to that the feeling that you're not getting anywhere sometimes, it's not surprising that some people give up or fail to put in enough time to improve their ability.

The term *practising* can have a negative feel to it, too – it suggests hours spent on your own, endlessly repeating exercises while everyone else is going out and having a good time. In any case, that kind of practice is not necessarily going to make for a good player.

So don't feel as if you're alone when you've just had enough or can't be bothered when it comes to practising. Everybody gets times like that. However, if you're like me, once I get started on something, I get into it and look forward to spending time on it everyday. And that's the crux of the matter – you might need to push yourself to get going, but once your interest is fired up, practising can become addictive.

As a professional, time spent with music is just what I do, and in fact I don't get nearly as much time to practise as I'd like. The reason I like to practise now is that I get a buzz out of learning and improving my abilities, because I know I'll never be able to reach a summit in playing – it's an infinite thing. The way that you'll get into practising is much the same. Once you feel improvement, and are able to put it into use, you start to feel the buzz and rise in self-esteem that goes with it. In life, we don't often get the chance to do things like that, sadly – at least, not with things that matter. With music, though, you're engaged in something artistic and creative, and that's a special feeling.

So when you need to motivate yourself to get up and spend some time with your instrument, think about these things. To be straight with you, doing something every day is the quickest way to improve – little and often, as I said in an earlier chapter. If you can get into this habit – and I mean half an hour a day upwards – you'll regard it as you would good posture and technique: it becomes a friend, a method of relaxation, that you can rely on. The only way in which you can't rely on it is if you're not bothered.

So, given this period of time of, say, half an hour, how is it best spent? Everybody's different, but breaking down your practice routine into areas can be a good idea.

Start off by getting comfortable, making sure that your posture is good and that you're relaxed and in control. A few exercises make for a good warm-up – you can refer to the ones in Chapter 2 and 3. Finish off with a few scales and arpeggios, maybe looking at a couple of keys you haven't done yet. That's a good half of the session gone.

When you're warmed up, look at a piece you want to play and work through it. Look at the chords, analyse them, see how the progressions move through different keys. Work through things slowly: if you start off playing something too quickly, the chances are it will always be scrappy. You need to train your muscles to perform new tasks when you play a new piece. You wouldn't take up running and immediately try to do a marathon, would you?

Don't forget to keep up your ear training. Listen to music that you know and try to hear what's going on. Find out what key it's in, see how the chords progress and are used. Through hearing music, you can learn so much, especially if you have in mind a lot of the things

I've talked about in this book. Don't shut yourself off from styles of music you might not like straight away, either – a good playing style comes from appreciating a diverse range of music. To be good at anything – blues, pop, jazz, whatever – takes understanding.

Finally, don't look down your nose at anything. Instead, respect it and understand what you can. Very few things are a waste of time.

My parting words with practising are therefore that, in order to make progress on your instrument, a certain amount of discipline is required, but not at the expense of maintaining your enthusiasm, so make it as interesting as you can for yourself. And, as one of my teachers used to say, 'Slow practice makes for fast progress.'

20 GOING TO AUDITIONS

Auditions are, to many people, the musical equivalent of a driving test – a nerve-racking ordeal that goes past in a blur and you're not sure how the hell you got through it. For the inexperienced, only a true exhibitionist goes into such a situation supremely confident.

And that's why people like that rarely get on. What you must realise is that the people in an audition room (normally the other members of the band) are just human beings like you and are probably thanking their lucky stars they're not the ones having to audition. Someone who goes in completely full of himself stands a much greater chance of failing than a person who just tries to be himself and does what he can do to the best of his ability. Most good playing jobs in the industry, such as touring and session work, go to people who are easy to get on and work with. Of course, in that environment, having a certain degree of playing ability is a pre-requisite, but not every professional player is a flash harry; instead, they make sure that they're easy to work with and good at what they do.

And that's what you've got to do. Think back again to earlier chapters – when talking about technique, I made the point that there's nothing wrong with having a simple but effective playing style. Your ability is going to be taken into account when you think about what kind of group or situation you might be getting into. It might be a little early to go for that avant-garde modern-jazz fusion outfit, but you might feel as if you could do a good job in a group where you can put into practice what you know. So, in short, don't be over-ambitious too early. There's nothing wrong with stretching yourself a bit, but remember that you learn something from most playing situations, however simple the music may be that you end up playing.

Don't be afraid of being a bit nervous: a bit of fear, an edge, in these situations can be to your advantage. Use it, regard the whole thing as a bit of an adventure, and above all don't ever think that this is going to be the only chance for you. There's always something else to get involved in if you don't feel right about things. You're not the only one on trial; they are as well.

If, as is most likely, you have to ring someone up about a place in a group, be honest about what you feel you can do. It's good if you have common ground, such as similar likes and dislikes in music – pretty helpful if you want to enjoy playing with them. They'll probably want to know what kind of gear you've got – again, be honest and don't feel inadequate if you haven't got a bank of keyboards to bring along. You might have to learn a couple of songs in their set to audition with, and if so, make sure you know them. Fairly obvious, you might think, but incredibly some people do go along to auditions with absolutely no idea of what they were given to learn. Give yourself plenty of time to get there, and if you don't hear from them afterwards, so what? Chalk it up to experience and look for something else.

21 TIPS FOR PERFORMING AND RECORDING

Nerves

All performers worth their salt – even the very best – get excited before going onstage. When they get out there, though, their minds turn to the task that lies ahead of them and they *focus*. This doesn't mean that the sense of excitement then disappears, but it does mean that they can control it and deal with it by concentrating on the job in hand, which is to give a *performance*. Come what may, they will play their instruments to the best of their abilities, and once they're onstage, that's all they'll think about. Sure, mistakes will happen sometimes, but that's occupying such a small space in their minds that the chances of it happening are small. Instead, they're focused on playing a piece of music from start to end, and that's it.

So, one of the golden rules about performing live is that you should never be afraid to make a mistake. That might seem like pretty crazy advice, but it's not as daft as it sounds. When I say 'never be afraid', I mean that you shouldn't waste time *worrying* about making a mistake; instead, accept that there will simply be times when you'll fluff a passage or play bum notes – even the greatest players do. Of course, the more you practise and the better prepared you are, the less likely you are to drop a note, but what distinguishes a good performer from a bad one in this respect is how they deal with it when it happens onstage.

When you do have a problem in a performing situation (and we're talking about maybe a few wrong notes or a wrong chord here), it's easy to lose your composure. This is partially born out of a subconscious need to acknowledge to the audience that you've made a mistake, and yet this is the very worst thing you can do, mainly because very few people will probably have noticed! When you practise a piece or a song endlessly, you familiarise yourself with it to a far greater extent than anyone in the audience will know it, so it often takes quite a major bodge for anyone to recognise an error, and even then your only thought has to be *to carry on as if nothing has happened*. If your overall performance is still good, people usually forget mistakes very quickly.

It's also a fact of life that some people feel more comfortable while performing than others. This doesn't necessarily spring from a natural tendency to be an exhibitionist, but is instead attributable to the confidence they have in their own abilities, which is a rather different thing. In this area of performing, there's no substitute to having a good physical relationship with your instrument, which you'll have developed through the process of getting really comfortable with new techniques, getting your form right and not rushing through new areas.

So don't take the attitude that nerves are things to be conquered; instead, make use of them. Take advantage of the extra edge they give you onstage, and adjust your mental attitude toward not worrying too much about mistakes. Provided that you've prepared yourself as much as you can (and only you can know whether or not you have), you should start to develop the ability to perform to your maximum ability, which is all part of stagecraft in general.

Coping With Recording

Studio recording can bring its own set of issues. In some ways, playing onstage can seem easier, because you have more leeway to make mistakes. Even if it's noticed, the audience's concentration will shift onto the next part of the performance. In a recording environment, however, what you play will be analysed more carefully and errors will be more noticeable. Some players enjoy the extra pressure that this can bring, but you should play it just as you would onstage: give a performance.

In these days of computer-based recording, it's pretty easy – particularly when recording via MIDI – to correct even quite heinous musical wrongdoings. You could even take things further and negate the need to play anything at all by instead programming the keyboard part directly from the computer. What this can't do, though, is give the recording its most important part: a human element. Sure, the more precise you are, the better, but it shouldn't be at the expense of putting in a musical performance.

Even if you're recording the old-fashioned way, using tape, there is still the possibility of inserting an *overdub* by *dropping* or *punching in* to record over just part of a take, which involves putting whatever multitrack tape-recording machine you're using into Record mode while the track is playing. This technique allows you to keep the good bits of a take while recording over something that needs correcting (provided that there's space) and dropping or punching out again. While using tape is less common than it used to be, it's still perfectly feasible to repair parts this way, if it's done with a reasonable degree of care.

Sightreading

Oh dear! If there's one thing that can make otherwise hardboiled musicians tremble at the knees, it's the prospect of having to sightread. This is a real shame, because an ability to sightread gives you the facility to experience and appreciate music you might otherwise never play.

Even so, many people look on sightreading as being a straightforward technical exercise, which is incorrect; it requires as much musicianship and intuition as any other aspect of performance. Good players who sightread well are sometimes accused by others of 'playing by numbers', almost as if good reading ability somehow presses a Bypass button in the musicianship department. Put bluntly, however, this is total crap; being able to sightread opens a door to a whole host of musical experiences. And if you're hoping to earn any money from your playing, you might well be expected at some stage to do a bit of sightreading.

While anyone can suggest techniques for improving sightreading, everyone has their own way of dealing with it, so here I'm just going to outline a few basic suggestions which I think might help. Beyond that, there's no real secret to it; it's just a matter of practising.

Being Put On The Spot

The worst possible scenario for anyone lacking confidence in their sightreading is being put on the spot, most commonly onstage. It's easy to forget when you're in this kind of situation that, in essence, you still need to give a performance. Of course, the more detail you can recognise, take in and play, the better, but the most crucial thing is to capture the *spirit* of the music. Therefore, sightreading becomes not just a technical exercise, in terms of reading the part, but a musical one where you use your ear, intuition and experience (where possible) to control the situation.

Nevertheless, you should always start by having a quick look through the part you're about to play, if possible. It's actually possible to take in a lot of information within a few seconds. Here are a few things to look out for:

- Note how long the piece lasts. Make sure you can find the end and that it looks complete – ie there aren't any hidden passages likely to spring out at you.

- What kind of piece is it? If it's a pop song, it may well have a simple structure centred around verse, chorus and middle-eight sections, which will often be either 8, 12 or 16 bars long. By relaxing and trying to feel the natural length of each of these sections, you can usually tell where it might go next.

- Note the tempo and the time and key signatures of the piece, as well as the type of notation used. A lot of songs start and end in one key, so think about what the relative minor or major key might be for the piece and look out for it cropping up. Also, try to make a note of the dynamic markings, as this will help you to start forming an idea of the piece in your mind.

- Most pop songs use a fairly limited selection of chords and similar rhythmic patterns, so keep your eyes peeled for areas of repetition. This kind of ability can allow you to scan through parts quickly.

- Likewise, look for areas that might cause problems. If the piece as a whole looks fairly manageable, use whatever time you have to focus on these problem areas.

Even taking all of these precautions, however, there will often be an unexpected surprise lurking ahead – a chord you might not expect, or a difficult-looking riff. This is where there really is no substitute for practice and experience. Even the most accomplished readers come across awkward sections at some stage, and when this happens it's up to you to use your musical instinct to help you out. Remember, it's the *spirit* of the part that needs to come across; sometimes you can get away with not playing all the notes in a certain chord or studiously playing all the smaller nuances of a part. As long as you keep going and maintain the tempo and basic feel of the piece, you should minimise problem areas.

The other valuable method of helping to cope with this is perhaps the golden rule when it comes to sightreading: *look ahead*.

Summary

The advice in this chapter will hopefully help you to develop a good overall approach to sightreading on the spot, but as far as your general sightreading ability is concerned, the more you do it, the better you'll be. This is something that applies to your overall musical ability too, of course, but it's even more true of sightreading; you really do need to practise it with a view to identifying notes and rhythms quickly. The time you spend at home, without pressure, just enjoying looking through new books of pieces and songs will be the main factor in developing your sightreading skills.

22 TURNING PROFESSIONAL

At some stage along the musical path, many people think about the idea of becoming a professional musician, and certainly some will be able to work themselves into a money-earning position. But as for a career as a full time musician... Well, I don't want to come over all negative, but it's a lot easier to earn a bit of money from music than to make a living from it. It's easy to get carried away after having made a few quid from gigging, and my advice would be, for most people, to keep your music as a pleasurable, part-time activity. Regard any income you derive from it as a supplement to your everyday profession.

The music industry can portray an unrepresentative image of lifestyle and expectations – at least for the majority of working musicians. Sure, a guy playing onstage with Sting is a professional musician, but then so is someone playing in the house band at Butlins for £35 a night. The reality can be somewhat different from the seemingly glamorous world presented by the media.

Additionally, relatively few musicians I know – including top session players – have earned what could be described as a good living year in, year out. They might have had good periods, but once the tour has ended or the album's been recorded, there are often long periods of inactivity, which translates as unemployment.

Further down the scale, for a freelance player, a regular engagement can be a rarity, and in any case is only seldom enough to get by. The fact is that simply being a paid musician is bloody hard work, and it can be incredibly stressful. As a career move, I'd hardly recommend it.

On the other hand, there are many good points to consider, some of which relate to any self-employed business. For instance, you decide whether or not you want to accept work (if you're lucky enough to be able to afford that luxury), and there's often a lot of free time involved – usually more than you'd like there to be! Crucially, though, like any other self-employed person, how well you get on isn't just down to how well you play or how much you know; it's down to how good a businessperson you are. The phone isn't just going to ring; if you want to find work, you need to put yourself about.

Playing And/Or Composing

There are two paths to be taken in this business. One is being a 'normal' earning musician – doing gigs, a bit of teaching, recording or whatever other sidelines you can find. You can do this right from the bottom level (playing in pubs and clubs) up to the higher echelons (touring and recording with signed artists). While you're unlikely to become rich this way, by being flexible and having a few sources of income you'll be giving yourself the best possible chance of earning a decent living.

The second path – which often encompasses a bit of the first as well – is to compose your own music and sell it. You could do this as a member of a group, as a solo artist or simply as a writer whose material is performed by other artists. If you can make it work, this kind of endeavour can launch you into an area of the business that can be highly lucrative. Look at most of the wealthy artists in the music business and they have all been, either individually or jointly, composers or songwriters.

The reason why there's so much money involved in this area of the music business is mainly because of the potential revenue within music publishing. Not in the paperback sense, you understand; in the music world, the word *publishing* refers to the royalties paid to a composer whenever his or her material is broadcast. At best, a hit song can earn a fortune for the writer. Lower down the scale, though, there are other opportunities, such as library-music or soundtrack work, areas in which many professional musicians manage to find work.

Being A Working Musician

So, looking at the first option, of being a basic earning musician without any particular ambition to go to the top of the scale, how good do you need to be? Straight away, we enter the paradoxic nature of the music business. As I explained earlier, merely being a good player doesn't necessarily translate into lots of work. It's that all-round situation again in which playing ability plays a large (although by no means exclusive) part. I would sum up the most important areas as follows:

Be A Good Person To Work With

This is somewhat obvious, maybe, but an ability to mix and get on with fellow musicians is a prerequisite. Working in a gigging or recording environment often means spending long periods travelling or hanging around. There's no need to be the life and soul of the party, just do the basic things right: be on time, be reliable and be easy to work with.

Have Reasonable Equipment And Make Sure You Know How It Works

As we'll see in later chapters, you don't need to spend a lot of money to get a good sound, provided that you can get the most out of what you've got. For starters, you'll need at least a couple of keyboards or rack units and, ideally, a small desk and keyboard amp. Keep them in good working order and invest in some flightcases to protect your gear in transit. A few gigs' worth of chucking electronic gear in and out of vans and you'll soon see the wisdom of protecting it.

Have Your Own Transport

If you don't drive, you'll need to learn. Gigging invariably involves having to get to inaccessible places at unsociable hours.

Put Yourself About

Making contact with others in the business, either through direct promotional means or (usually better) through introductions from fellow colleagues, is your lifeblood. If no one knows you're there, they can't ask you to do anything.

Getting to know people can initially be a bit of a daunting task. In this respect, a local music scene can be the easiest way to start to get around. Look for advertisements placed in local music shops, rehearsal rooms and newspapers by covers bands looking for keyboard players. (Lots of free-ads papers also run adverts like these.) Get to know the people who run the local rehearsal rooms and recording studios. Nothing may come of your efforts for a while, but your name will soon get around if you work on making yourself known. If you can play solo, approach a few restaurants or bars that stage live music.

When you've found a few working situations, don't stop there. Hopefully, the grapevine will yield a few calls from people requiring your talents, but don't rely on this. Keep searching and maximising your chances of obtaining work.

Look Presentable

Like it or not, the way you look will have a direct bearing on the kind of work you're likely to end up doing. If you want to be a working musician, the likely venues at which you'll be performing in – such as clubs and function rooms – will mean that you can't be too outlandish in your appearance. You've got to look right for the kind of work you want to get, and for the purposes of this particular example, you'll need to project a more restrained image than you might prefer.

That said, however, adopting a trendy and arty look can be a definite plus in certain areas.

Moving Up The Scale

If you want to be a bit more ambitious and try to get session work playing for name artists, this requires a somewhat different approach. Most of this kind of work comes from word of mouth, so the wider your circle of musician friends, the better. When you enter this more elevated area of the business, factors such as image and equipment become even more important; you've got to look as if you could realistically be in a band that goes onstage and performs at big venues – and this applies not only to your appearance but also to your confidence in performing in such a situation. Again, playing ability isn't necessarily the sole criterion at work here; many session players are good, solid musicians who perform and move around well onstage.

Aside from your own contacts, you might want to approach agents who fix musicians for bigger name artists. You can sometimes find lists of these in media reference books in your local library. Remember that your presentation must reflect the kind of work you're going for, and this means you'll need to get a really good professional picture taken, along with – ideally – a CV or brochure and a quality CD that shows off your playing abilities. And even then, don't expect to have a high rate of reply; you might well get none.

Composing Music

Selling your own music can be one of the most satisfying experiences in the business. It can also be one of the most frustrating, as not only are openings hard to come by but you also face a lot of competition from other groups or individual writers.

For many people, writing outside a group situation is likely to be more applicable, so I'll concentrate on giving advice to anyone who wants to compose either on their own or maybe with a co-writer.

Your first job is to look at the genres open to you – songs or instrumentals – and decide which suits you best, then condense this list further and decide on specific areas. For instance, looking at songs first of all, many writers focus on composing pop tunes with a view to them being taken up by artists who don't write their own material. If successful, this can be a particularly lucrative area, although very competitive. The key to successful writing is in supplying the right material for a particular genre, so if this is where you want to earn your cash, study the musical area you want to write for and hear how sounds and production styles work in conjunction with that particular genre of music.

Recording

When you have the bare bones of what you think might be a promising track, record a version at home first of all (and if you're serious about this, you'll have invested in a reasonable home recording setup – which, again, doesn't have to be expensive) and hone it until you have a version that you think works. If you can't sing it yourself, pay a session vocalist to perform it for you. Remember, you're essentially recording a demo here, but if you think it's worth it, you might want to record it in a higher-quality studio than your own to give it that extra bit of polish that might get you noticed. Again, however, time is often the critical requirement in recording, and if you can't afford enough hours in a better studio, you're often better off recording your material at home.

Publishers

Once you have the completed CD in your hand, the people you really need to contact are those music publishers who have influence and clout in the industry. You can easily find out who these are by looking at the credits section on any big-name CD. The question then is, will they take you seriously?

This is unfortunately where you're on your own, and your success in this area is largely down to how good at business you are. All I will say is this: If a publisher hears a CD full of material he thinks could be a hit for someone, he'll take an interest in it. He'd be a fool not to. Getting it to him, and being taken seriously, is the hurdle you have to overcome. As is so often the case, persistence is the key. Keep sending out new recordings, always improving your material and learning new techniques and avenues of distribution. It can take many, many rejections or non-replies before you're successful in placing material you've composed. Many give up without any success at all.

Instrumental Music

Instrumental music has a rather wider market than vocal music. In addition to film, TV, advertising and library music, the world of multimedia opens up many new doors, such as the computer-game industry. In this field, the quality of music produced has increased substantially in recent years, and again there is a lot of competition between fellow composers. (Many good games musicians are often out of work.)

Library music, meanwhile, is usually commissioned directly from specialist publishers, and your (by now well-used) media reference book will tell you who they are. Again, you need to find the right kind of sound to succeed with library music – it's often used behind commercials or within TV programmes created with only a small budget for music. Watch satellite daytime channels for examples of shows that use this kind of material. You'll find that this type of music often needs a slightly quirky yet inoffensive quality in order to be effective; just as the pop song is crafted with technique as well as inspiration, so too is library music. And the same things apply here as elsewhere: you need to make contact and persevere in order to have any chance of success.

To find TV or film work without prior experience is difficult. In addition to the above, you need to have a pretty good technical knowledge of music, production and recording to have a chance. Many people start off by writing library music as a stepping stone to these more lucrative areas, and I'd recommend this route unless you're really confident in your abilities. If you're successful in finding a publisher who is prepared to place some of your library music on TV, this can be very much to your advantage when trying to find a way in.

Summary

So, to sum up, there are no straightforward ways to get on in the business. Even if you're exceptionally talented, you'll almost certainly need to be flexible regarding the kind of work you're prepared to do, and most successful professionals have a number of different revenue streams. However, it can take only one phone call – often completely unexpected – for something to change. A lot of the best work I've had has occurred this way, sometimes through people I'd met only once or twice, so if you're determined to follow the life of a professional musician, remember that. And, above all, don't stop trying!

Part 2

Getting Technology To Work For You

23 WHAT KIND OF GEAR DO I NEED?

This is one of the questions I get asked most often, and it's possibly the hardest to answer. It can be broken down a lot, though, by simply asking yourself, 'What kind of music do you want to play?' If you predominantly play piano music, occasionally trying out other musical directions, then a home keyboard or electric piano may contain enough features and sounds to satisfy your needs for a long time. On the other hand, a synthesiser keyboard will offer a much wider range of usable sounds and more flexibility, should you wish to expand your musical directions. Then, of course, you could maybe do with an electric piano and a synthesiser to cater for both eventualities. Welcome to the world of lusting after bits of musical equipment you can barely afford!

As well as a choice of piano sounds, an electric piano will usually have a limited selection of other instrument sounds on board. These are typically along the lines of strings, organ and, possibly, bass. I've often found that most of the effort has gone into making the pianos sound good and that the other sounds are something of an afterthought. While this isn't always the case, if having a large selection of high-quality sounds is your priority, I would consider a more general-purpose keyboard instead, or as well.

Aside from this choice, the only pre-requisites I'd place on equipment would be that it needs to have a MIDI interface, ideally with a General MIDI capability, and – in the case of a synthesiser keyboard or module – it should be multitimbral. These features are pretty essential these days, and even if you're not entirely sure what they mean, any reputable shop will steer you in the right direction. The chances are that, unless the keyboard/module in question is veering on the vintage side (over ten years old), it should be both multitimbral and MIDI-equipped.

How much do you have to spend? The fact is that these days most modern equipment is pretty amazing. The last decade or so has brought such an advance in technology that you don't need to spend very much money to get a keyboard or rack module that has excellent sound quality. The issue then becomes not so much what you have, but how can you get the most out of it?

24 THE ESSENTIALS

Essentials – what could they be? Well, just like in playing, there are different areas to know about within the technical side of electronic music, and sometimes it's assumed that you know what someone's talking about when in fact you haven't got the faintest idea! So, here's a brief nuts-and-bolts run-down of a few basic need-to-knows.

First, you need to know the leads that connect your keyboard. There are three primary types: mains, MIDI and audio.

Mains Leads

The unit will have either an integral cable or a socket at the back where you connect usually either a two-pin or three-pin lead. Three-pin leads are normally called *Europlugs* and are the same as you'd find on many kettles. Two-pin leads are the sort you'd connect up to your shaver or many portable hi-fi units.

MIDI Leads

We'll come to what MIDI is about very shortly. To be

able to identify a MIDI cable, though, is an extremely basic thing – it's a lead with a five-pin DIN socket on each end.

Audio Leads

These come in a few shapes and sizes. If your keyboard has integral speakers and amplifier – such as most electric pianos and home keyboards – you won't need to connect any audio leads to make a sound. However, if you need to connect it to a source of amplification – to play with a band, for instance – you'll need to look at the outputs it has and connect it up the same way as you would a synth keyboard. A synthesiser doesn't normally have any built-in amplification at all (although you can use headphones).

Commonly, there are two types of output socket found on keyboards. Most usually – and almost certainly with a synthesiser keyboard – it will be a quarter-inch jack socket (it should be marked as 'Output' somewhere on the panel nearby). If you're having trouble finding the socket, it's about the same diameter as a drawing-pin head. A standard jack socket will be mono, characterised by one ring on the lead tip. Some electric pianos, however, have phono sockets, not jacks, for output. These are the same as you'll find on the back of a piece of hi-fi such as a CD player, and they're easy to recognise, as they're smaller than jack leads.

Connecting Up To Make A Sound

Now, what do connect your keyboard to? There are many options here, but we'll concentrate on two, firstly with an amplifier that's designed for the purpose. A typical keyboard amp would be a *combo*, meaning that the amplifier and speaker are all in one unit. Using one of these is simple: you just plug the jack lead from your keyboard into it and turn it up. If your keyboard has a phono output, you'll need to buy a small connector to plug into the end of your phono lead, which will then plug into the jack socket.

The other option is to go through a pair of hi-fi speakers or proper studio monitors. You can put your keyboard through your hi-fi amplifier – and thus your speakers – by connecting the output of your keyboard into a spare input on the back of the amplifier (maybe the 'Aux' socket) and turning it up. If your keyboard has a jack output, though, you'll conversely need to buy a small connector to plug onto the end of the jack lead to go into the amplifier, as most hi-fi sockets are phonos.

basic Keyboard Workout

Most equipment these days can run in stereo or mono. Look at the output sockets on your keyboard – you may well have one with 'L' above it and another with 'R', meaning 'left' and 'right'. Both need to be connected if you want to hear what you're playing in stereo. The easiest way of doing this is through your hi-fi. You may have noticed that the input channel on the back of your hi-fi amp had two sockets, one white and one red. Connect the left output of your keyboard to the white socket of the amplifier and the right output to the red one.

If you're using a combo amp as described earlier, you'll need two of them to hear your keyboard in stereo. This is because the left and right outputs of your keyboard both need to be connected to a separate speaker (your hi-fi does this because the white, or left, socket is routed only to the left speaker and the red, or right, socket is routed only to the right speaker).

If you can run your gear in stereo, do so, because it almost invariably sounds better. In a rehearsal or gigging situation, where you may only have a single combo available, there are still ways around this – once we've looked at a few other issues first...

25 MIDI AND MULTITIMBRAL KEYBOARDS

Earlier, I advised that any keyboard you buy should have a MIDI interface and be multitimbral. I'll now give you an introduction to what these things mean and what they can do for your playing and enjoyment of music. The important thing is not to be afraid! Take them one step at a time and you'll find that these are very exciting things to learn about and to put into practice.

What Is MIDI?

You can't hear it and you can't see it, yet it's probably the most important development in electronic music. These days, virtually every piece of musical hardware, such as a keyboard or effects unit, has a MIDI interface built in, and even if you play a basic home keyboard, those five-pin sockets are your gateway to a new world of musical experiences.

In spite of this, or sometimes because of it, many people are slightly fearful of exploring what MIDI can do. It's actually an incredibly simple facility, and I'm going to show you how useful it can be. First of all, I'll explain how MIDI (Musical Instrument Digital Interface) came into being and illustrate some of the things for which it can be used.

Rewind to the early 1960s. Electronic music was in its infancy and synthesisers were built around analogue, pre-transistorised technology. You may well have seen pictures of early synthesisers – huge pieces of metal hardware the sizes of a bookcases spewing forth myriad spaghetti-like leads. Tiny piano-type keyboards would be connected to these monstrosities in order to play them. By the end of the 1960s, an American inventor by the name of Robert Moog took advantage of the development of the transistor to design much smaller synthesisers (such as the classic Minimoog) which were also considerably cheaper.

Minimoogs and similar units from rival companies became extremely popular and started to feature prominently in pop and rock music. There were drawbacks to these early keyboard synths, however, the main one being that, due largely to their analogue control interfaces, they were *monophonic* (ie they could play only one note at a time).

Fast-forward to the end of the 1970s and things were

looking a bit different. Some keyboards could now play several notes at one time (ie they were *polyphonic*) and digital technology was becoming cheaper. The yards of spaghetti described earlier could now be replaced by digital circuits and control panels. Before the end of the decade, the first entirely digital synthesisers had appeared.

With these advances, there was an opportunity to design an interface that would enable digital equipment to communicate with other, similar units and be used and controlled from a single source – a single keyboard, for instance. Rather fortunately, the various manufacturers all decided on a common system to allow this to happen and MIDI was born. Consequently, from the mid-1980s onwards, virtually every keyboard, from humble electric piano to top-of-the-range synthesiser, has been built with a MIDI interface.

The MIDI Effect

Without explaining any more, let's pitch straight into a real-life scenario. You have two keyboards: Keyboard A and Keyboard B. Each has a MIDI interface.

You go to your local music shop and buy a standard five-pin MIDI cable. You plug one end into the socket marked 'MIDI Out' on Keyboard A. You plug the other end into the socket marked 'MIDI In' on Keyboard B. Providing both keyboards are set to the same MIDI channel, and both are connected to an amplifier and speakers, when you play any note on Keyboard A, the same note on Keyboard B will sound as well. When that note is played on Keyboard A, you're generating a MIDI signal, which is transmitted through the MIDI cable to trigger Keyboard B. (Of course, this is not limited to one note – you can play any number of notes or chords in this manner and MIDI will transmit them all.)

Notice that Keyboard A is acting as the *controller*, and that the cable is plugged into the MIDI Out. That's because you're playing a note, and therefore sending information out of Keyboard A, and that's why the cable is plugged into the MIDI In of Keyboard B, the *slave*, as it is receiving information. This basically explains two of the three MIDI sockets you commonly find on the backs of keyboards. We'll come to what the other socket, 'Thru', does in a moment.

It is important that you understand what MIDI is doing here. It does not transmit *sound*; it transmits *information*. In essence, when you play that note on Keyboard A, it is sending a message through the cable to Keyboard B, telling it to play that same note. If you turned down the volume on Keyboard B and triggered again it from Keyboard A, it would still receive the MIDI message but would not make a sound. You would have to turn up Keyboard B again to hear it, just the same as if you were playing it directly. All the MIDI signal is doing is remotely controlling Keyboard B.

Because of this ability to control other instruments and devices from a single keyboard, it is common these days to buy *modules* – versions of keyboards that come in a standard rack-mounted form – with no integral keyboards. All the sounds and features of the module are exactly the same as the equivalent keyboard, and all its functions – note information to make it sound, as well as other MIDI data – can be controlled from the master keyboard. This saves space in a studio or live environment. Modules are so popular now that several don't have keyboard equivalents.

The above is a very simple example of what MIDI can do. Its usefulness spreads much wider than merely triggering notes on another keyboard. After all, a MIDI message such as that note information is basically data – binary code – comprised of os and 1s. Most keyboards can transmit other messages as well as note information – for instance, if you changed a voice on the controller keyboard, it would send a message through the MIDI cable to the slave keyboard and the slave would also change voice accordingly (if set up to do so). The same goes for movements of the pitch-bend and modulation wheels and the sustain pedal. In fact, just about anything you operate on a modern keyboard can be sent out as some kind of MIDI message.

Using MIDI To Record Music

However, you're not limited just to sending information to another keyboard. This is where MIDI gets really interesting. As I said at the start of the chapter, virtually all modern musical pieces of electronic equipment have MIDI interfaces. These days, most computers also have facilities to receive MIDI signals, and by using sequencer programs they can be used to record and play back MIDI note information.

Some keyboards have sequencers built in, although these are often of a fairly limited capability. More usually, a sequencer will either be in hardware form (a small metal box) or software form (such as the computer-based program mentioned above). While hardware sequencers were popular in the early days of MIDI, most sequencing is now done on computers, for a number of reasons.

As an example, though, I'll use a hardware version to describe the basic operation of a sequencer. A hardware sequencer would typically be about the size of a large A4 book, have a row of buttons with transport controls (Play, Record, Fast Forward and Rewind) and a MIDI interface, with MIDI In and MIDI Out. That's all we're concerned with for now.

Referring to the earlier example with Keyboards A and B, we're going to leave the MIDI lead in Keyboard A's MIDI Out socket but remove it from Keyboard B's MIDI In. We're going to put it into the MIDI In of the sequencer instead. Therefore, the keyboard is still our controller and we're going to send out note information through the MIDI Out socket. The sequencer is going to receive this information through its MIDI In.

While normally you would set a tempo on the sequencer, that isn't actually necessary for the purposes of this example, so all that's needed to record music is now to check that both the keyboard and the sequencer are on the same MIDI channel and to press Record on the sequencer. Whatever you now play on the keyboard will be transmitted through the MIDI cable to the sequencer and stored as note information (data) within the sequencer. (Remember, MIDI deals with information only.)

When you press Stop on the sequencer, you'll want to hear your masterpiece back. However, the MIDI connection is going out from the keyboard into the sequencer. To hear back what you've recorded, you'll need to connect another MIDI cable (or swap around the original if you were too broke to buy two), this time going out of the sequencer and into the keyboard. Then, provided that they're both on the same channel, when you press Play on the sequencer, it will transmit the note information you recorded onto it back to the keyboard, and the keyboard will play.

26 MIDI CHANNELS AND SEQUENCING

When explaining how basic MIDI situations worked in the previous chapter, I made reference to MIDI channels. MIDI has 16 separate channels, all of which can transmit and receive data simultaneously, independently of each other. Within the scope of what I've already illustrated, there seems little point in having 16 channels – surely just one would do?

The simple fact is that we've only scratched the surface of what MIDI can do. When you start to explore multitimbrality, you're opening up another new area of possibilities and you'll soon understand the need for more than one MIDI channel. In fact, it will become clear that 16 are often not nearly enough...

Multitimbral literally means 'many sounds' and describes the ability of a keyboard, or module, to play back several sounds at the same time. A modern synthesiser, for example, has a substantial array of sounds, from pianos through to basses, brass instruments and drum kits. With a multitimbral keyboard, you can assign up to 16 different sounds and record and play them back on any of the 16 MIDI channels. In order to do this, you need to use a sequencer, and these days the easiest and best way of doing it is to hook up to your PC or Macintosh.

You see, the simple hardware sequencer I looked at in the previous chapter isn't the most user-friendly thing around. Often the only display you have on these models is a tiny screen, and in terms of computing power they're way behind what modern computers can do. So, if you haven't bitten the bullet yet and tried making music with your PC, then now is a good time to start. The chances are that it will involve only a very minimal amount of expense, and it will take less time to get comfortable with it than you thought.

Hooking Up To A PC

One of the problems of a book like this is that there is often a wide disparity between equipment at people's disposal. One of the key issues where computers are concerned can be whether you use a PC or Mac. Lots of people within the industry use Macs, and many people have them at home, too. However, I suspect that most of you will be using a normal home PC, at least at the moment, and while advice is relevant to both PCs and Macs, there are some operating differences which may crop up when using a Mac.

The power of a modern PC is more than enough to supply all your likely needs for recording at this stage. Anything above 400MHz with a hard drive of 10Gb should be sufficient – ample to give you space to store recordings. Obviously, the damned things get quicker all the time, so even a fairly recent model can be OK.

The very basic operation of a music sequencer program is similar to standard word-processing programs you may have used on a computer before. Some of the menus at the top will be the same – File, Edit and Help(!) – so you can get a feeling for your surroundings quite easily. But before you're able to start recording and playing back files, we need to look at what kind of hardware you have on your computer.

The most essential thing you need right now is a means of getting a MIDI signal in and out of the computer. Unlike a standalone sequencer computers don't have built-in MIDI sockets, so your computer will need to have a soundcard, a device that enables you to plug your keyboard into the computer. A lot of computers have built-in, integral soundcards which will do the job for now. You will need to buy a cheap 'Y' cable, one end of which will plug into the soundcard's joystick port. On the other end of the cable will be a pair of MIDI leads which you connect to your keyboard. Put the cable marked Out into your MIDI In and the cable marked In into your MIDI Out.

If your soundcard is properly installed, you should have enough hardware connected to be able to start basic MIDI recording. Other methods are available, such as using a USB device, but we'll come to these later.

Programs

Again, one of the difficulties with this subject is that things change so quickly and new programs come out all the time. I'm going to give you enough information on the type of program you need to use – a multitrack sequencer – to get you started and get you to appreciate the multitimbral capability of your keyboard, if so equipped. Even if your keyboard is not multitimbral, you can still get a lot of use out of the sequencer, so read on.

When you've loaded the sequencer program and it's running on your desktop, if you play a note on your keyboard it should register as being received by the sequencer. This will probably be in the form of a little bar lighting up as you depress and release the note, just to reassure you that it's connected and working. Most programs have a series of vertical tracks running from top to bottom of the screen, and in the default setting that these go to when first loaded, they'll probably select track 1, which will also usually be set to MIDI channel 1. Your keyboard, unless you've altered it, should also be set by default to MIDI channel 1. Therefore, with everything on the same MIDI channel and a MIDI signal being received, you can start recording.

Put the program into Record mode and play a few notes. When you've finished, stop the program. (Most scroll horizontally when playing back or recording, so something should have appeared on-screen when you were recording.) Now press Play. Provided your keyboard is connected to an amplifier, you should hear what you recorded.

Again, you must understand what's going on here. Your computer is playing back only note information – it hasn't recorded any audio. The audio you're hearing is coming out of the keyboard's output socket, just as if you were playing it. The computer is playing back the note information you recorded into it, through your keyboard. If you used a sustain pedal, your computer will also have recorded the information generated when you depressed and released it – this is a type of *controller information.* Each control change you make on the keyboard, be it via sustain pedal, pitch-bend or modulation wheel, patch change – in fact, just about anything – has a dedicated controller-information number and can be recorded onto the sequencer, either as you play notes or afterwards, when your computer's playing back.

So now you have a track to play back on the sequencer. To add to it, check that the sequencer isn't set to replace the track and you can record another part on a different track, as long as the MIDI channel is adjusted to 1 – you'll then hear both. However, this is a little restricting, as you'll have selected only one sound. To go further, you need to get into multitimbral operation.

Multitimbral Operation

First of all, this requires you to take a closer look at your keyboard. As I've explained, some older keyboards may not have this facility, nor will a lot of electric pianos or home keyboards. Multitimbral synthesisers started to appear in the late 1980s, but some equipment produced much later may still have only a limited facility.

At its best, multitimbral capability enables you to assign a different voice to each of the 16 MIDI channels over which your keyboard can transmit and receive. Some earlier or lesser machines may have enough power to assign up to only six or eight voices. That doesn't necessarily matter too much.

A multitimbral keyboard usually has two modes it can be set in for normal playing. One is often called *Patch mode*, whereby you select the various sounds the instrument has, one at a time. The other is called *Performance mode*, and in this mode you can start to assign several different sounds at once. This is a slightly different procedure, depending on which manufacturer's keyboard you're using, but the principle is the same. You will be able to select up to 16 *parts* (each with a different sound, if you wish) within a single performance and give each of them whichever MIDI channel you desire. (It's possible to give them all the same channel, if you want to.)

Now, for the purposes of this exercise, assign part 1 to a piano sound and set that part to MIDI channel 1. When you go back to your sequencer, make sure that the track selected is set to MIDI channel 1, and you can play and record exactly as you did before.

Set part 2 on your keyboard to a bass sound, for example, and to MIDI channel 2. Select or create a new track on the sequencer set to MIDI channel 2, and when you record the bass part you'll hear the piano part being played back on channel 1 at the same time. The parts are completely separate from each other, just as they would be on a multitrack tape recorder. You can then do this with up to 16 sounds, enabling you to create or play back a very full-sounding track.

27 GENERAL MIDI

Fairly early on in the days of MIDI, it became clear that, even though the basic principle of controlling other manufacturers' instruments via a MIDI interface worked, several details needed to be ironed out. One of the most typical was the difference in patch-numbering systems between different manufacturers. As I've explained, when selecting a patch on the controlling instrument, the slave also changes, if set to do so. All very well, but the only problem was that patch numbers between different makes of instrument weren't universal. Patch 10 on a Roland keyboard wasn't the same sound as patch 10 on a Yamaha, for example.

This made the construction of MIDI files particularly awkward. In theory, if every manufacturer used the same patch numbers for the same sounds, a track could be made up on a sequencer, with appropriate program and patch changes, and it could be played back on any multitimbral, MIDI-equipped keyboard. As we can see above, this was beset by inconsistencies between different makes of keyboard. A lot more standardisation was necessary to make this a reality, and so the idea for General MIDI was born.

With manufacturers agreeing to standardise patch numbers to certain sounds and create a recognised sound set, where a standard was set for 128 patches to appear in a certain order, under the new General MIDI protocol it was now possible to create compositions that could be saved on a MIDI sequencer as GM files and played back on any GM-equipped keyboard, irrespective of the manufacturer. The one requirement was that the keyboard used to play back the GM file was fully multitimbral; in other words, it could receive and play back 16 MIDI channels at once, each with a different GM patch. So, if playing back MIDI files is a priority for you, ensure that the instrument you buy is fully multitimbral.

Listening to other people's MIDI files can be quite good fun, and useful, too. When you import a MIDI file into a sequencer program, it's handy to see how they've programmed the song. Of course, the quality of files varies enormously – you can, at one extreme, buy professionally produced MIDI files that are made to a very high standard, while at the other you can download an endless number from the internet. If you are doing this – and most musicians have done at some point – bear in mind the usual provisos about viruses and hidden content, particularly as the file will come as an attachment.

28 CONNECTING INSTRUMENTS VIA MIDI

The third MIDI socket on your keyboard can be used in a number of different ways. Taking our initial, basic example from Chapter 25, where we controlled one keyboard from another using a single MIDI cable, a further keyboard can be controlled by linking it through the slave unit's MIDI Thru socket. This third keyboard can then be controlled in the same way as the original slave. This daisy-chain method can be further extended to include other MIDI-equipped devices.

Basically, the Thru port passes on all the information that comes into the MIDI In socket and transmits it to the next device. If you're considering using two or three MIDI-equipped devices on a regular basis, you may find it worthwhile considering a multiple-port MIDI interface, which will make your life a lot easier. Honestly!

Multiple-Port MIDI Interfaces

If you have only one keyboard, then you're unlikely to need more than the 16 MIDI channels we've already encountered. However, if you have more than one instrument, or even just another MIDI-equipped device, such as a drum machine, then you may soon realise the limitation of having just 16 channels. Let's presume that you have a couple of keyboards and have used one of them to recorded a track that uses all 16 MIDI channels. This means that, if you wanted to record another few MIDI tracks using the other keyboard, there would be no spare channels.

Fortunately, there is a way around this. The method of connecting your keyboard that I described earlier – using the joystick port – usually works OK but is limited in that it restricts you to 16 MIDI channels. These days, a separate USB MIDI interface is worth looking at because it's cheap, easily installed and can offer a number of separate MIDI ports. A USB MIDI interface is a small box that simply plugs in to one of the USB ports on a computer at one end and, at the other, has a number of MIDI sockets to which you can connect your equipment. Most USB interfaces of this type have more than one 'port', meaning that you have multiple (usually at least four) MIDI Ins and Outs, meaning up to 64 MIDI channels. You can select which port to use on the sequencer program.

The beauty of this arrangement is that you can have

one keyboard set up permanently, and once it's connected you can use it to control other MIDI gear without having to plug and unplug MIDI cables. With a USB device, the proviso is that your computer has to be switched on in order to power it, but the chances are that it would be anyway if a sequencer program was being used (and some run on batteries as well).

29 SETTING UP YOUR GEAR

At some stage, many of you will want to put into practice what you know and start rehearsing with a group and performing on-stage. This brings its own set of issues, both practical and technical.

Setting Up Your Keyboard

For rehearsal purposes, in order to hear yourself it will be necessary to have something along the lines of the combo amp discussed earlier. These models have the advantage of being very self-contained, so all you need to do is plug it in, connect a jack lead from your keyboard and turn it up to get a sound. They should also be loud enough (I'd get something around 100 watts) to hear what you're doing in a rehearsal room while a guitarist is wailing away and the drummer is knocking pieces out of his kit.

However, when you get to a gig situation, things may be quite different. Obviously, a gig situation can be anything from someone's front room to a small club, a theatre or a larger venue. In anything apart from the smallest gigs, your combo won't have enough power or projection for you to be heard. In these circumstances, a PA (Public Address) system will usually be provided, so that you and the other members of your ensemble can all be heard. PA systems vary enormously in size and capability, but they all follow the same principle – a set of speakers each side of the stage, pointing out towards the audience, through which the band is heard. Very small PA systems are sometimes suitable only for vocals, but in most circumstances they will be big enough to put your keyboards through.

So, how does this happen? Well, there are several ways to cook this egg. Your combo will almost certainly have a Line Out socket somewhere on it called a DI (Direct Inject), and a lead can be taken from that and given to the PA engineer. This sends a feed from your combo to the PA. However, this way you're not making the most of the sound of your keyboard – it's in mono and you're restricted in how much you can turn yourself up on-stage, because whenever you turn up you will correspondingly send more signal out through the DI socket to the PA, possibly causing distortion problems and earning you an earful after the gig.

In my opinion, there's a better way, allowing you to

retain as much control over your sound as you need and still ensure that the signal getting to the PA is of as high a quality as possible. However, some very modest expenditure is necessary.

I'd suggest you purchase a small mixing desk – one with either six or eight input channels would be perfectly adequate – which has at least one auxiliary send (I'll come to that in a moment). Most mixing-desk manufacturers make such models, and they are usually of good quality and useful in several other situations as well as live performance.

Such a desk will be very easy to use. Whether it has six, eight or more input channels, typically it will have a fader for each input channel and a fader on the right-hand end to control the master volume. Some very small 'notepad'-type desks don't have faders, only knobs, which is OK, but using these is sometimes less immediate when things are dark on-stage and you need to adjust something in a hurry.

Input channels are easy to understand – each one can have a single mono input plugged into it, such as a lead-out from your keyboard or a microphone. An input channel will usually have the following controls (from the top of the channel downwards):

- **Gain** – If this is turned to zero, you won't hear a sound. Turn it up slowly to increase the level of your instrument coming into that channel;

- **Equalisation (EQ)** – Typically, this comes in the form of three knobs marked High, Mid and Low. Use these in much the same way as those on a home hi-fi to change the tone of the sound (if necessary);

- **Auxiliary Send (Aux)** – The desk may have one or two of these knobs. As the name suggests, it sends out the signal from that channel to allow connections to be made to another piece of equipment (I'll come to this in a moment);

- **Pan** – Used to control which side of the stereo speakers you want that sound to come from;

- **Fader** – Brings up the volume level of a channel;

- **Master Fader** – Controls the overall volume of the desk.

One of the advantages you may notice straight away with a desk is the ability to run in stereo. Most keyboards sound infinitely better in stereo – if in doubt just listen to it on headphones. If your keyboard has a straightforward left and right output you can put the left one into desk channel 1, for instance, and the right one into desk channel 2. Provided they are both turned up to the same level, the only thing you'll need to do to make sure these run in stereo is to turn the pan knob on channel 1 all the way to the left and the same knob on channel 2 all the way to the right. That way you have only the left output of the keyboard sound coming through the left side of the desk and the right output coming through the right side of the desk. To connect your desk to the PA plug a pair of leads into the master output sockets on the back of your mixing desk and give them to the PA engineer. Make sure he knows you're running in stereo.

Plugging in a pair of headphones into the desk can be very useful as a way of hearing what's going on, particularly when needing to tell if you're running in stereo or mono.

Hearing Yourself On-Stage

The next question is, how do you hear yourself? You've plugged your keyboard into your mixing desk, given the outputs of your desk to the PA engineer and your expensive combo amp is lying in the corner feeling sorry for itself. Well, it's still going to be used, but it will have to be connected in a different way to the way it was before. This is where you'll find that the auxiliary-send feature is indispensable.

Usually called a 'send' or 'aux', the auxiliary send enables you to feed a separate signal from your desk to the combo. On the rear panel of the desk, there will be a socket marked 'Aux' or 'Aux Send'. If the desk has more than one auxiliary send, for these purposes just use aux 1. The Aux socket on the desk is usually a normal jack type – connect a jack lead from this Aux socket to your combo. Make sure the combo is turned up.

Presume that one of the outputs from your keyboard is going into channel 1 and that you can hear yourself through the main outputs of the desk (using headphones would do), turn up the Auxiliary Send knob on channel 1 and you should hear it coming out of your combo. You can adjust the level of send on the desk or the volume on your combo to make it louder or quieter.

Any changes you make to your Auxiliary Send knob won't alter the levels coming out of your desk's master output. The auxiliary is a completely separate feed. Therefore, in this way you can make the most of your stereo sound by giving your mixing desk master output to the PA and still have complete control over your own volume on stage.

This type of little desk can be extremely useful. At home, you can connect up the master outputs to your hi-fi and run several instruments through it in stereo. Spare input channels can be used to plug in other instruments or microphones as well. It's possible to pick up a new desk that will do the job for anything between £80 and £200. Second hand, they can go for peanuts.

30 SAMPLING

It's fair to say that sampling has permanently changed the face of music. However, the term *sampling* is used so widely these days that many people are unsure of what it actually means. Sampling simply allows you to record something digitally and then play it back by means of triggering sounds from a keyboard or (more typically these days) via a sequencing program. Whether you have some or no knowledge of the subject, it's very useful to understand how early sampling was achieved and how it has evolved into today's vital tool.

Sampling Development

It's comes as no great surprise that advances in sampling have gone hand in hand with the development of digital technology. For instance, the first moderately useful hardware samplers were developed in the early 1980s, when digital systems and circuits began to become more available.

Two of the most popular early samplers were the Fairlight and the Emulator. The Emulator, in particular, looked just like a regular keyboard, despite its wealth of sound-producing capabilities. What you could do with it, though, was revolutionary at the time: you could plug an instrument, microphone or indeed any sound source into it with just a regular jack lead, then press the Record button on the Emulator and it would digitally record whatever you played into it. You could then play back the sound using the Emulator's keyboard. And, of course, you could record absolutely anything you liked – a piano, a vocal line, a drum groove, someone speaking or a dog barking – and if you listen to a few '80s synth bands you'll hear that they *did* sample just about everything.

You could also play back the samples on the Emulator's keyboard at varying pitches. However, the higher up the keys you played, the faster the sound, which gave a Mickey Mouse effect similar to that involved with speeding up a tape. Conversely, the lower down the keyboard (below the pitch of the original sample) you played, the slower the sample would be. This effect was often quite a large problem, depending on the type of sound that had been sampled, but the overall result was the same: the tone and character would be changed if you went more than a few notes above or below the original sample. The answer was to make several samples of the sound – for instance, when sampling a grand piano, you would take a sample every fourth or fifth note to give a realistic sound when playing back the sound on the sampler. This technique is still used today, and is a process known as *multisampling*.

So far, so good. But while the Fairlight and the Emulator were both pioneers of a new technology, they were, in their original forms, impractical and of rather limited abilities. Firstly, they were both prohibitively expensive (particularly the Fairlight) and handicapped by having only a small amount of memory. This meant that only a short sample time was available, and as all of both machines' onboard data was lost when they were switched off, samples had to be saved onto removable disks (which had nothing like the capacity of today's storage media). So they were initially niche machines usually bought by wealthy artists or expensive studios, who could offset the time (and cost) needed to load and save samples.

The Digital Age

Technology develops at a frightening rate, however, and on the horizon were digital samplers for the masses, machines that could be bought at reasonable cost and gave ordinary musicians a chance to try out this revolutionary new technology. While there were several initial attempts, the first really groundbreaking sampler was the Akai S900, developed in the mid-'80s. Designed as a keyboardless module equipped with a MIDI interface and a form of multitimbral operation, it helped to spawn a new generation of musicians who made history by sampling and producing records in their bedrooms. At the time, there was no other remotely effective competitor, which meant that the Akai brand name became synonymous with samplers in general. The company continues to develop its sampling instruments today.

However, while it might have opened new musical doors, the S900 was still a relatively limited device. It could sample only in mono, and the total amount of sampling time that the onboard memory could support was only something like 20 seconds at a reasonable bandwidth (don't worry, this is explained later). While it would allow you to perform basic editing tasks such as looping (where part of a sample is played and then replayed and replayed, *ad infinitum*, in order to save memory) and making up multitimbral patches of samples, it wasn't long before more highly developed versions eclipsed it.

Nevertheless, in many core respects, the modern samplers available today are merely more powerful, more highly developed versions of the S900. They all operate on the same principle in that, once you've sampled a sound, you can then edit it on the sampler by deciding which bits of the sample you want to keep and then storing them, either on a floppy disk, on an internal hard drive (similar to the one on a home computer) or on some other format, such as a Zip drive.

Generally, the kinds of tasks for which people use hardware samplers like these are twofold. One is to sample a selection of notes from another instrument and use those to create a *patch* (or sound) that can be played just like a sound on a regular keyboard. The other is to sample sections of music – a drum groove, for instance – and use this to make up the basis of a rhythm track by triggering it at the start of each bar. Traditionally, this is one of the most widely used methods for making up dance tracks.

But sampling, and indeed recording in general, has moved on a lot in recent years. While hardware samplers still have their uses, there is now a much neater way of recording digitally, one that uses a household object we've encountered already: the home computer.

31 RECORDING MIDI AND AUDIO WITH A SEQUENCER

We've looked at how it's possible to hook any MIDI-equipped keyboard up to your computer, given the right hardware. The type of software you need to use here is called a *multitrack sequencer*, of which there are many different brands and types, the most popular being Cubase VST and SX (made by Steinberg) and Logic (made by Emagic). While there are operating differences between the two, they both do the same thing: allow you to record and play back MIDI information. If you have a multitimbral MIDI keyboard or module, you can use it to record several separate tracks with different sounds and then play them all back together, making up a very full-sounding track. However, in addition to recording MIDI information, Cubase, Logic and most modern multitrack sequencers can also record audio data. The audio tracks can then be viewed on the main Arrange page of the program, along with the MIDI tracks, which makes it very easy for you to see instantly what's going on, as all the tracks scroll across the screen horizontally while you're playing.

basic Keyboard Workout

There are several advantages in recording certain types of audio using your computer rather than a hardware sampler. Firstly, audio uses up a lot of memory, and while a modern hardware sampler is infinitely more powerful than the old S900, it can't hold a candle to a desktop computer's performance. Secondly, any audio you record on your computer is stored instantly on its internal hard drive, making it a much quicker and more straightforward process.

Perhaps most relevantly, however, the array of processing and editing functions that a desktop computer and sequencing program allow you to perform on an audio file provides you with a much greater degree of flexibility than you could possibly get from a hardware sampler. You can speed the file up, slow it down, copy and paste it, apply processing such as equalisation to it – the list is endless.

So here we'll have a look at how to get audio onto your computer, and how to use it in conjunction with the MIDI tracks you can record using your keyboard.

As with MIDI, a computer needs an interface in order to allow it to be connected to audio equipment. This is usually a fairly painless procedure, as most computers are sold with an adequate soundcard. While you can spend a lot of money to get a soundcard with a superior audio specification, a cheap Soundblaster or the like will do perfectly well to get you started.

At the back of the card will be a selection of audio sockets (often mini-jacks, in the case of cheaper soundcards). One of these sockets will be designed to accept audio in, while another will send audio out. Both will be stereo sockets, so you might need to acquire specific cables to connect up your audio source to the card. You can then run your soundcard's outputs through your hi-fi or (better) a mixing desk to hear the audio.

Sampling Rates And Disk Space

Once you've connected everything up, take a look at the Preferences or Setup menu in your sequencer program. There will probably be an option there to choose which sample rate you wish to use.

Like anything else, audio always requires space in which to be stored, whether this is on a cassette tape or on a computer's hard drive. When audio is recorded digitally, the amount of memory or hard disk space it uses up is determined by a few key factors, such as whether the audio is recorded in stereo or mono; whether it's recorded at 16-, 24- or 32-bit resolution; and the sampling rate (measured in kHz), or the number of times the signal is measured per second. All these combine to determine the quality of the recording.

CDs use a sampling rate of 44.1kHz, and while I wouldn't recommend using a rate lower than this, it's still a perfectly acceptable number. Likewise, a lower resolution than 16-bit can result in a noticeable drop-off in recording quality. Higher sampling rates, such as 96kHz and 192kHz, are appearing increasingly often on better-specified soundcards, but you should be aware that not only do these higher rates gobble up more space on your hard drive, but you might also be hard pressed to hear the difference.

Starting A Recording

Before recording audio onto your sequencer, first of all you should name the track, after which you can select whether it's to be recorded in stereo or mono. Most programs also have a Mixer page where it's easy to tell whether or not an audio signal is being received by your soundcard. If it is, you should be ready to record a few bars. Put your sequencing program into Record mode and off you go.

When you stop playing and press the Stop button on the sequencer's graphic interface, the audio track will probably appear on the Wave Edit page as a squiggly wave-like graphic. This image actually describes the data quite accurately, because part of the process of recording audio onto your computer requires it to be converted into a digital waveform. This audio file is now stored on your hard drive, and you can do what you want with it – save it along with the main song, delete it, re-record it or edit it. The number of audio tracks that your sequencer can handle will depend upon several factors, including the quality of your hardware, but most can manage up to 16 mono tracks quite comfortably.

While there are many more avenues to explore in the field of audio recording, you should by now have a mini-recording studio at your disposal.

Dealing With Files

Audio files are usually saved as either of two specific types. If you use a PC, they will be saved as WAV files, while on a Mac they will be stored as AIFF files. Most Macs can read WAV files and convert them into AIFFs, just as PCs can convert AIFFs into WAVs. In either case, though, at the end of the day they're computer files, which means that you have a vast range of possibilities. We'll look at some of these in a moment.

Before we do, though, let's try to get this whole process of dealing with computer recording – both MIDI and digital audio – into perspective. Whenever you deal with digital data, it's just that: data. You already know that MIDI is just a form of information, that it's not sound itself; essentially, it's just a string of numbers telling a bit of gear that it has to perform a task, which could be anything from playing a note to changing a sound. When audio gets recorded onto your computer's hard drive, it's converted from (usually) an analogue signal into a digital waveform – which, again, is merely data. To be heard as music, it has to be played back using a specially designed program (such as a multitrack sequencer) and fed out of the soundcard to an amplifier and speakers.

As you probably know from using standard word-processing programs on your computer, you can do an awful lot with data – cut out bits of it, copy it, paste it or put it into other programs that read the same type of file format. While an audio file might be a hell of a lot bigger than a text file, it's really only a different type of computer file. When you fully take this concept on board, it makes it much easier to understand how it's possible to do so much with digital audio.

Let's go back to the audio recording you did a little while ago. After you stopped the sequencer, the track should have appeared on the main Arrange page as a segment, just like a MIDI track. Within this Arrange page you can move the audio track around to your heart's content, dragging and dropping it into any part of the song, or by copying and pasting it to a different location. It's not hard to realise that this kind of editing functionality can make constructing a song a very simple matter and can open up a wide range of possibilities.

Processing Audio Files And Plug-ins

Now we're really starting to get into the area where the power of your computer starts to become a major factor. The term *audio processing* refers to the alteration, or treatment, of an audio track, and over the years audio processing has become an integral part of recording. The most basic, and common, types of processing are some that you might already have encountered – effects such as reverberation, echo/delay, equalisation, chorus and so on. Many of today's keyboards come with onboard effects like these which you can apply to the instrument's sounds, whereas just a few years ago the only effects available were boxes of outboard gear, separate units that usually stood in an impressive-looking rack case, each of which had to be connected up to a mixing desk (or other means of feeding a signal in and out, such as an effects loop on an instrument amplifier). As well as consuming a lot of physical space, the useability of separate units like these was restricted if you didn't have a large enough mixing desk to run them all at the same time.

In addition to the aforementioned basic effects, there are countless other forms of processing available, and we'll be looking at these at a little later on. What you need to know now is that the power of a modern computer allows you to do away with these separate effects boxes, if you wish. You can now process all of your audio within your computer by applying digital effects to the audio tracks in the sequencer program. While this hasn't exactly made outboard gear redundant, most of it now caters for the higher ends of the market, because being able to process audio within a computer is easy, convenient, and it works pretty well.

You'll find that some effects will be contained within the sequencer package, while you can also import other effects, known as *plug-ins*, which will run alongside your sequencer program. The procedure for finding an effects (or *FX* for short) section in a sequencer package will vary from program to program, but there will usually be an FX button on the screen near where you would type in the name of the audio track on the Arrange page. Clicking on this will normally launch a separate window providing various options concerning which effects you want turned on or off and the amount of level you want to send to each one. (You can normally select a range of effects from one of the main menus that drop down from the top of the page. Try 'Panels' or 'Options'. If you get lost, refer to the user manual for guidance.)

The principle here is to get you started, so I won't go into too much detail about using the various forms of FX. For now, just experiment and see how many different types of sound you can produce. There's one thing you'll notice fairly quickly, though: the drain that using onboard FX has on your computer's processor. The fact is that audio processing requires a lot of memory and computing power; the more audio tracks you use, and the more FX you use, the quicker you'll notice a slow-down in general computer operation to the point where, in extreme circumstances, the computer will stop playing the sequencer entirely. Most modern computers can take on a very high workload before they do this, but while using FX can be fun and can transform the sound of even quite humble recordings, it's worth remembering not to overdo it.

We're going to return to this area and look more closely at making music once we've had a quick look at integrating all this equipment so that it works for you.

32 A QUICK TOUR OF THE STUDIO

While the prospect of being able to do so much within your computer can be exciting, it can sometimes be restricting to work entirely in the virtual domain, so I'd always recommend using a mixture of hardware and software, for reasons I'll come to shortly.

It's impossible to get away from the fact that one piece of hardware at the heart of a good setup – in the studio or live – is the mixing desk. We looked closely at using a desk to give you a good live sound using a small six- or eight-channel version with two auxiliary sends. As we're exploring the area of recording again here, though, we're going to look at slightly different types of desks, which, although larger, still operate on much the same principle.

You can find yourself needing some sort of desk at quite an early stage in your recording. While it's possible to use a separate keyboard combo amp, or to run the signal straight into your hi-fi, as soon as you need to connect up more than one or two pieces of equipment and hear them at the same time, you're sunk. And this serves as a good illustration of the role of a mixing desk: it's a meeting place, a junction, through which many pieces of equipment can be heard at the same time. When you get deeper into audio recording, though, you'll soon find out that you need rather more than this.

If you want to record two tracks of audio onto your computer using a basic desk, it's quite simple. You take an output from either the main stereo outs or the auxiliaries and plug the cables into your soundcard. However, you have the capability on your sequencer program to record many more than two audio tracks at a time, and you might also want to record one instrument on one track, another on a second, mix two or more channels onto a third – an infinite amount of possibilities exist. In short, you need to be able to send different sounds to your computer out of separate outputs.

This requirement for a separate output section determined the make-up of mixing desks long before computers were used to make music. The common configuration of an input section (like that on a small live desk) and a separate output section (known as a *subgroup*) became a popular choice for sending out signals to multitrack tape recorders, and is still the basis for the construction of recording desks today. Of course, desks come in all shapes and sizes, right up to the massive models you see in the top studios. But, whatever the size, a recording desk will work on the same principle: in addition to its input channels, in order to be truly flexible, it must also have a subgroup section with separate outputs.

Analogue And Digital Desks
Analogue Desks
The small live desk described above is classed as an *analogue* desk, which means – from a user's point of view – that each function has its own dedicated control, be it a knob, slider or button, which makes this type of desk relatively easy to understand and get to grips with.

Typical home or small studio recording desks are split up into three sections – input, subgroup and master output – with, for instance 16 input channels, eight separate subgroup output sockets and a stereo master output section. The input sections on most models are in most respects identical to those on many small live desks (described in more detail in *Part 1*), apart from one main feature: each input channel will have a row of numbered buttons which, when depressed, send the signal in that numbered channel along the desk to the equivalent output socket. You would then need to run a lead from that output socket to your computer soundcard. For example, depressing button 1 would send the signal to the first separate output, button 2 would send the signal to the second, and so on. Of course, you can send the same signal to all eight separate outs if you want, or a combination of signals from any of the 16 input channels, in a process known as *routing*, or *assigning*. It's a very flexible system, ideal for multitrack recording.

Digital Desks

The digital desk is a slightly different animal. For a start, it's a bit smaller than its analogue cousin, with very few knobs on the front panel; instead, the various controls of the desk are accessed via a series of onscreen menus. This makes simple things like adjusting equalisation and panning a little less intuitive than on an analogue console, though not as hard to get used to as you might expect.

Where the digital desk *does* score is in terms of features. The analogue desk doesn't usually contain any significant means of processing a signal, requiring you to connect up separate outboard gear, whereas the digital desk usually has a substantial array of onboard effects that can be applied to any input channel. Not just the basic reverb, delay and chorus, either – often more serious studio tools, such as compression and noise gates, are also thrown in for good measure.

The other trump card that a digital desk offers is its ability to save and recall mixes. Digital desks allow you to save complete *snapshots* that memorise positions of faders, EQ, effects – virtually everything. So, if you want to move between songs that have completely different settings, you can save a mix and move on to the next one knowing that you can recall your saved mix at any time.

When it comes to a separate subgroup section, a digital desk often has several options. Instead of having a series of output sockets, digital desks have slots on their rear panels which allow you to insert cards containing various types of interface. You can opt for a traditional series of analogue input and output sockets, or you can use a digital card that accepts digital XLR, optical or coaxial cables. Like most other features on a digital desk, assignment is done via a series of menus, which personally I don't mind, although many prefer the more visible, hands-on approach you get with an analogue desk.

Hooking A Desk Up To A Soundcard

So we now have a means of getting a number of separate signals out of a mixing desk, ready to be recorded. How far you can now go depends on the specification of your soundcard. A cheap Soundblaster-type card, as described earlier, will get you started with basic audio recording, but it will probably have only one stereo input, so if you want to take in the separate outs from a mixer, you'll need to purchase a (slightly) more expensive card that will accept multiple inputs. Currently, these cards can be found from around £100 ($180) upwards, and typically they will accept series of either analogue inputs (the leads coming from your analogue mixer's subgroup section) or digital cables.

Digital recording interfaces come in many different formats, two of the most popular consumer varieties being A-DAT (which uses two optical cables, one in and one out) and TDIF (which uses two coaxial cables). With these digital interfaces, you just plug two cables into the input and output sockets on the digital card at the back of your mixer, then plug the other ends into their respective sockets on your soundcard. Each cable can then carry up to eight tracks' worth of recording data.

- **CAUTIONARY NOTE!** Either your soundcard or your mixing desk (but not both) must be set to send out a Word Clock signal, which can be carried through the cables already connecting the two devices. Failure to do this properly will result in the signal being corrupted with glitches and pops, which can spoil your recording.

So, as you can see, while you'll need a digital mixer (and a soundcard with a digital interface) to connect up to your computer digitally, you can still hook up quite happily with an analogue desk.

Opinions vary about the relative merits of analogue versus digital recording. Personally, I think there are far too many factors involved to get into that debate here. However, the ability to recall mixes and the onboard effects present on digital desks can make them a more suitable choice for use with a computer music system. That said, though, you should never underestimate the ability of older equipment to do a good job.

Effects And Processing – A Quick Breakdown

These days, digital processors and effects can be found on board mixing desks, on your keyboard, as computer plug-ins and as outboard gear, and what follows is a brief list of some of the most common effects:

- **Reverberation (Reverb)** – This is perhaps the most widely used effect in both live and recording situations. Natural reverberation occurs when sound carries around large internal spaces, like cathedrals, bouncing off the hard reflective surfaces so often the reflections blur together. (I could have said 'echoes' rather than 'carries', but echo refers to another specific effect, which shouldn't be confused with reverb.)

The reverberation in a cathedral is an extreme example, as it lasts for several seconds, but a digital reverb program or unit will contain patches that can replicate anything from long reverb times like this to very short, almost imperceptible ones. The most common use of reverb is to add a little depth to a sound, sometimes without it being very apparent. Indeed, many keyboard sounds benefit from a moderate amount of reverb – but be careful not to overdo it when applying it to regular sounds.

As well as varying the reverb time, it's also possible to alter the mix of the reverberated and original, 'dry' signal in order to increase or decrease the amount of reverb heard.

- **Echo** – Also known as *delay*, this effect often gets mixed up with the wrong terminology. The effect of echo, or delay, being applied to a sound is most easily understood by imagining yourself in a situation where the sound bounces from one surface to another, such as a cave or a valley; if you called out, the sound of your voice would be repeated several times, in a distinct number of echoes, before dying away.

  While many years ago studios used to use complex analogue echo units, modern echo-type effects are created by digital delay programs. A digital delay works, by, in effect, sampling the incoming sound and repeating it. Delay times can be selected from long to very short, with longer settings giving the effect of the sound being produced in a cave or valley and shorter settings producing slapback effects. A feedback control determines the number of times the delay repeats.

  Digital delays also have a feature known as a *modulator*, which can be used to create several other effects, such as chorus.

- **Chorus** – This is an effect designed to fatten up a sound by modulating it – ie by making the pitch waver slightly above and below the note. As the original dry sound is overlaid with this chorused effect, it can give the impression of more than one instrument playing, because of the constant but very subtle variation in pitch. You can vary the speed and depth of the chorus effect to give a greater or lesser effect as you desire. Chorusing can work very well on synth-string parts – particularly higher up the keyboard, where some string sounds can start to get a little weedy – and a slow, wide chorus can give extra width and depth to sustained sounds such as organ and brass patches.

- **Phasing** – Phasing effects can also be created by using the modulation feature in a delay program. The term *phasing* refers to the sound that results when two identical sounds are played simultaneously, placed 'on top' of each other. In the old days, two tape machines were run in synchronisation to achieve this, but today it's a simple matter to use a delay program to produce the same effect. Using a very short delay setting, you can mix the processed and the original dry sound to create a very distinctive sound. Slow rates of modulation particularly suit sounds such as string pads and ambient effects.

Compression

Compression is one of the less glamorous-sounding processes, but it's nevertheless a tool that's worth its weight in gold. Like many other pieces of electronic music gear, at one time compressors were all separate, stand-alone pieces of hardware that sat in racks. These days, compressor plug-ins are amongst the most widely used and popular forms of processing. To understand why, and what one can do for you, you first need to know some of its typical uses.

The dynamic range of most musical instruments and voices can be extreme, and in a recording environment (and, sometimes, live) levels that are either too high or too low can potentially ruin the sound. Most of you, I'm sure, will have heard an overloaded signal when you've recorded a tape at too high a level, or the lack of presence when the recording level has been too low.

A compressor's job, very generally, is to compensate for this by reducing the level of a sound when it has reached a certain point. This can both prevent distortion and also help to deal with a difficult, peaky sound without the overall level being too low. In short, it squashes the sound into a smaller, more manageable dynamic range.

A compressor can be applied to a single channel or an overall mix. Either way, basic controls do the same job:

- **Threshold** – Sets the point at which a compressor starts to reduce the level of a sound.

- **Ratio** – When a sound has exceeded the threshold and compression is kicking in, the larger the ratio, the more compression will be applied. Ratios can be selected from 1:1 (no compression) to infinity:1 (at which point no signal whatsoever will be allowed past the threshold point). When a compressor is used at this latter setting, it is performing the task of a limiter.

- **Hard/Soft Knee** – When a sound reaches the threshold, hard-knee compression is applied to all of the signal straight away, whereas soft-knee compression is introduced gradually, before the threshold is reached, and is often a more musical, less obviously compressed sound.

- **Attack** – Determines how quickly the compressor reacts when a sound has exceeded the threshold.

- **Release** – A user-defined release time can be applied to determine how quickly the compressor's level returns to normal when the sound has fallen below the threshold.

Compression can actually be a surprisingly creative tool; setting a slow attack time, for instance, can allow part of a percussive sound – such as a clav – to pass through uncompressed, accentuating its sharpness. While it's primarily a studio-based animal, compression can also be applied effectively to individual channels or the master output of a mixing desk when playing live.

33 SOFT SYNTHS AND SAMPLING

We've already looked at some of the basic means of getting a MIDI signal into and out of your computer by using either a cable attached to your soundcard's joystick port or a more dedicated unit such as a USB interface. Once this has been done, it's then possible to record MIDI signals onto a sequencer program and output them via MIDI to whichever sound source you happen to be using.

However, there are a number of other sound-generating options that can be used in conjunction with your computer. One of these involves using software synths, or *soft synths*.

Soft Synths

A digital synthesiser, in its hardware form, uses digital waveforms to recreate a wide range of sounds. In many ways, it makes sense to put this digital information onto a software disk and run it from your computer, thus giving you the 'guts' of the physical keyboard synth (ie the mathematical data used to create various sounds) without having to clutter up your studio with large pieces of equipment.

While some soft synths come as complete stand-alone programs, the ones described here can be controlled from within the same sequencing program you use for normal MIDI and audio recording. In this instance, they will typically appear as options on your MIDI Track Output menu. You can then send a MIDI signal into the computer by playing a keyboard to trigger the soft synth. The synth will also have its own Edit panel, allowing you to make up and tailor your own sounds, thus bringing you ever closer to integrating your studio within your computer. It's also a fact that soft synths are significantly cheaper than their hardware counterparts, although in practice there's a wide variation of success with which various soft-synth packages work.

One problem is the sounds they produce. In theory, it should be possible to recreate the sound of any synthesiser ever produced, and yet some soft synths are distinctly better in this field than others. Soft-synth designers often favour trying to replicate the sound of some of the really old analogue synths from the '60s and '70s, which is an appealing idea because, as very few good examples of these instruments still exist –

and they were all designed long before the days of MIDI – a soft synth equipped with these kinds of patches provides a great opportunity to use classic sounds in a modern environment.

The thing about older synthesisers, though, is that their older circuitry and occasionally stroppy behaviour were what gave them character and a unique type of sound, and these idiosyncrasies are captured better by some soft synths than others. The huge range of different soft-synth products out there can give you a massive library of sounds, though, and there are many really good-sounding products currently available.

The other major issue at stake is latency, which we'll come to in a moment.

Soft Samplers

Recording audio into your sequencer program is one way of integrating MIDI and audio within your computer, while another is to use a software sampler. There are many occasions, too, when a sampler fits your requirements far better than sequencing sections of audio.

As you might expect, a software sampler works on the same basic principle as a soft synth, using the processing power – and, in this case, the hard-disk capacity – of a desktop computer to give a very powerful and flexible alternative to a hardware sampler. It's integrated in much the same way into a typical sequencing program, such as Cubase or Logic. While a soft sampler will also have a separate menu for sampling, it should appear as a playback option in the same Track Output menu as a soft synth.

However, the way in which a soft sampler works is a little different to the hardware versions looked at earlier. On a hardware sampler, when you start recording, the sample is saved into the machine's internal RAM (Random Access Memory), which can be accessed very quickly so that, when you play a note, the sample associated with the key can be heard virtually immediately. The downside of this setup is the relatively small amount of RAM afforded by most hardware samplers, limiting the total sampling time available.

When a soft sampler records a section of audio, the data is stored straight onto the computer's hard drive, just as it is with audio sequencing. As the size of even the smallest computer hard drive is many, many times greater than the internal RAM of a hardware sampler, it's possible to record extremely long samples – in theory, right up to the capacity of your hard drive. When you want to play back these samples, they're read back from the hard drive in a process known as *streaming*. However, the computer's hard drive won't be able to respond quickly enough when a note is played (there's a short but noticeable delay before the sample can be accessed), so a small amount of the sample is loaded into the computer's RAM to compensate for this.

This gives you the best of both worlds: instant playback response and the huge storage space of your computer's hard drive. It sounds like a great way to approach sampling, and in many ways it is, although again you have to bear in mind the potential drain on your computer system.

Latency

Latency refers to the delay that's incurred between playing a note on a keyboard and hearing the required sound generated by a soft synth or sampler through a speaker or headphones. In severe cases, this latency can be serious enough to make playing very difficult.

Latency is largely a product of the buffer on your computer's soundcard. A large buffer size can help the card handle demanding situations, often when the computer is heavily loaded with various tasks. To get the lowest possible latency, however, you need to reduce the size of the soundcard buffer to as low as you can get away with. This will vary from computer to computer, and can only be done by trial and error, although, given the computing power of most modern systems, you should be able to achieve a latency of under 11 milliseconds, which will make any delay virtually unnoticeable.

However, you should be aware that, by lowering the computer's buffer size to achieve very low latency, you'll also be making computer less able to deal with occasional hiccups whenever its processor is heavily loaded. This can cause glitches and imperfections in a signal and a degradation of audio recording quality. As with most things, there is a compromise involved, I'm afraid, and here it is.

Saving Your Work

You can tell that your particular system is approaching the edge of its capabilities when it gets less and less responsive. It may even stop altogether. However, you can't always tell when it is going to crash. The more applications you have running at once, and the more your system struggles as a consequence, the more prone you are to this calamity.

If you're using soft synths and samplers, you have the added pain that they will all go down as well, so whatever you do, get into the habit of saving your files regularly.

Using Sampling CDs And CD-ROMs

One of the big advantages of having a good computer-based music system is that you can use thousands of commercially available sample-library discs containing samples that you can load into your audio sequencer or sampler, whether it's a hardware or software model.

These discs tend to fall into either of two categories: the sort that feature drum loops, vocal licks, ambient noises and other generally useful samples, and dedicated multi-disc libraries of orchestral instruments that have been painstakingly recorded. These latter library discs can be frighteningly expensive, and are specifically designed to be used with the sort of streaming soft sampler described earlier. The former, general library CDs tend to be reasonably cheap, however, and can be a great way of getting hold of sounds to put a track together. Most contain WAV files that can be imported straight into a track on your sequencer, so they're very easy to use out of the box.

34 BASIC PHILOSOPHY OF USING GEAR

When you're using any kind of recording gear, the kind of equipment you end up using is largely a function of what you want to do – and, of course, the size of your budget. It seems inescapable that computers are fast becoming the centre for most people's musical needs, and, as we've seen, using sequencers, soft synths, soft samplers and plug-ins means that you can now do more within your computer than ever before.

However, while everyone finds their own way of working, my advice would be to avoid putting all of your eggs in one basket. Sometimes we expect too much from a computer – whether this is through running too many applications or using software that doesn't quite manage to do what you want it to – so my advice is to be aware of what you can get out of all of your equipment – including older, semi-obsolete gear – before buying the latest soft synth or processing plug-in. Older equipment isn't generally worth much anyway, so unless you really need the space, hang onto it because it might come in useful one day.

What counts is your approach to sound and, more specifically, the degree of control you can have over each device. At the end of the day, the only connection you have with all of the audio programs and sounds on your computer is through your soundcard, which might have only a limited amount of outputs. It's this fundamental factor that can make a big difference to the sound of your recordings.

This is why you're best off with a physical, hardware mixing desk at the centre of your setup. Sure, sequencer programs such as Cubase and Logic have onboard facilities allowing you to adjust the levels of each MIDI or audio track and make adjustments, but there are drawbacks here. Firstly, unless you can permanently bring up the mixer in a separate window (which is sometimes possible), you have to go into a menu and select it. Secondly, these selections have to be made onscreen, so you have to use your mouse or keyboard to make adjustments, which isn't a particularly hands-on way of doing things. Thirdly, on an onboard mixer, while you can apply EQ and effects to each audio track, it'll start to use up your system resources. And finally, of course, you might also be sending out MIDI information to several keyboards or sound modules, which all need to go through some kind of mixing system in order to be heard.

With this being the case, I recommend that you share out the duties a little. Using a hardware mixer (either analogue or digital) has several advantages. While the size of the model is determined by your own requirements, basically a 16-input-channel desk with an eight-channel subgroup section should give you quite a bit of room to expand. Inputs have a habit of being used up surprisingly quickly; many synths and keyboards, for example, have separate outputs in addition to their stereo ones, all of which need to go into separate input channels on your desk.

Once you've got the signals running into your desk, you can then apply EQ, panning or effects using the auxiliary sends. It's this control of separate outputs that can be a major factor in improving your sound.

You can also return the outputs from your soundcard back through the input channels on the hardware desk. If you have multiple outputs, this can eat up your input channels, making you appreciate the benefit of having a reasonably sized desk very quickly! The advantage with this way of working, though, is that you then have other options for mixing the audio tracks from your computer. While these tracks can still be adjusted from the sequencer's onboard mixer, returning them through a hardware desk means that you have more hands-on control (if you desire it) and you don't need to rely on the computer to do everything; you can use the EQ and processing on your hardware desk instead, taking some of the burden away from your computer's CPU. If you can afford a digital desk, you can also use it to memorise your mix settings, which can really add to your system's flexibility.

You should therefore consider the following when you're deciding on how to set up your system:

- If you agree that a hardware desk is a good idea, try to obtain a digital one. It's possible to find good, useable, second-hand examples for around £500 ($900) or more, and if you're lucky you can find one that has a recording interface as well for that money.

- The performance of a computer is so dependent on the hardware fitted to it that it's impossible to give a good minimum specification. However, if you can, try to get a system that has been specifically designed for music use. You then stand the best chance of getting a well-matched system with good soundcard performance.

basic Keyboard Workout

- Don't throw away your old gear for the sake of it, unless you absolutely have to. You might need it some day.

- If your keyboard is limited in sounds and facilities, consider purchasing another keyboard or module before looking at soft synths. Having something physical to play and operate can make your setup more flexible, which will help when something breaks down...

- Learn to get the most out of your current gear in addition to looking at new avenues. Understanding techniques such as using separate outputs and learning how sounds work with each other can lead to your music having a new lease of life.